THE TRANSFORMATION OF AMERICAN SOCIETY

Progressivism, Multiculturalism, Tolerance

THE TRANSFORMATION OF AMERICAN SOCIETY

Progressivism, Multiculturalism, Tolerance

Linda C. Raeder

Sanctuary Cove Publishing
Palm Beach and Richmond

Library of Congress Cataloguing-in-Publication Data

Raeder, Linda C.
   The Transformation of American Society / Linda C. Raeder.
   Includes bibliographical references.
   ISBN 13-978-1544-7792-25
Typeface: Garamond Pro

In loving memory of my father,

Howard M. Maxwell

Contents

Acknowledgements

I am indebted above all to the many students at Palm Beach Atlantic University who participated in my courses in political philosophy over the past sixteen years. This work would not appear in its present form without the knowledge and understanding I have gained through my experience teaching undergraduates at PBA, and especially those enrolled in my Freedom and American Society and Roots of American Order courses. I would like to thank all those students who shared their perspectives and insights over the years and provided indispensable feedback to the ideas presented in this work.

I am further indebted to the PBA administration, particularly President Bill Fleming and Dr. Ken Mahanes, both of whom have provided unwavering support and encouragement for my scholarship and teaching. My colleagues in the Politics Department, Dr. Francisco Plaza and Dr. James Todd, have also earned my deepest gratitude, not only for their graciousness and collegiality, but also for the penetrating insight and maturity of vision that mark their scholarship and teaching.

Thank you as well to my mother, Evelyn Raeder Maxwell, for her steadfast love, support, and strength, and my dear animal companions, Max, Sophie, Callie, and the Muscovies, who make day-to-day existence a continual joy.

THE TRANSFORMATION OF AMERICAN SOCIETY

Progressivism, Multiculturalism, Tolerance

The truth does not cease to exist because it is ignored.

—George Orwell

The modern ideological movements—communism, socialism, fascism, and related constructs—were driven by persons who desired fundamental transformation of Western society. Movement leaders well understood that the "change" they demanded required transformation not only of established political, economic, and legal institutions but also the values, beliefs, and traditions that constitute their ground. Carriers of the ideological impulse understood, in particular, that the radical expansion of governmental power central to their vision was unlikely to be achieved in a society saturated with traditional religious commitments. Western Christianity is fundamentally at odds with totalitarian or unlimited government of any form. Indeed Christian thought and practice in the West led to development of precisely the opposite concept— limited government, limited as temporal government inevitably appears in light of the eternal life anticipated by the Christian faithful. The Judeo-Christian conception of moral law—an objective and higher law rooted in divine authority—establishes further intrinsic limits to the power of government, as does the historical Christian differentiation between the related but distinct realms of God and Caesar. Government is conceived not as the source of law or rights but rather administrator of a pre-existing moral law that binds ruler and ruled alike, and whose authority is confined to its legitimate sphere. Traditional Christianity, moreover, turns a granite face to the lure of worldly or political salvation—the explicit or implicit promise of modern secular messiahs of all stripes—and rather condemns worship or divinization of

1

the state as idolatry. It regards salvation as individual or personal salvation through the grace of God, not collective salvation through the secular state. For such reasons and others, modern ideologues aimed their guns, figuratively if not literally, directly at biblical religion. Such a strategy is true of Comte, Marx, Stalin, Hitler, Castro, and others.

The attack on the Judeo-Christian tradition, however, was not restricted to the more virulent expressions of the ideological impulse, such as communism and Nazism, but joined by sympathizers and fellow travelers of various stripes. English movements such as Fabian socialism, positivism, and the "advanced liberalism" of J. S. Mill, as well as American counterparts such as Progressivism and Social Gospel, shared many goals with their more radical brethren, as well as the assumptions, beliefs, and motivations that informed them. The chief differences between the two camps concerned strategy, not substance. The main such strategic division was the preference of Anglo-American variants for democratic gradualism over violent revolution. A second difference relates to the degree of socialization or collectivization advocated by either camp. Classic Marxism advocated overthrow of the free society in toto—limited government, capitalism, private property, rule of law, customary morality—and its replacement with totalitarian communism. The Anglo-American variants aimed to replace the free society not with outright communism but rather a managed or planned economy ordered by political elites or "experts" believed to possess knowledge unavailable to the common man. The classic communist and socialist vision has been explored in previous chapters. The present chapter examines its ideological cousins and fellow travelers, the less virulent but equally influential Anglo-American expressions of the modern and postmodern collectivist impulse.

The Transformation of American Society

Progressivism, Social Gospel, Secular Humanism

The chief carrier of nonviolent collectivist aspirations in the American context was the so-called Progressive Movement that rose to prominence at the turn of the twentieth century. Early Progressivism had broad political appeal, encompassing both Republicans and Democrats, both Theodore Roosevelt and Woodrow Wilson. Its central belief, shared by partisans of all stripes, was that "Progress" entailed an ongoing adaptation of existing social institutions to time and circumstance. History, argued the Progressives, does not stand still and neither should the institutional structure of society. Social institutions, most pointedly, should evolve in accord with historical change. Only thus may a society achieve the "living" institutional and interpretive frameworks essential to its Progress. Progressives were particularly concerned to adapt American political principles and practice to the flux of history. Traditional conceptions embodied in the vision of the Founders, especially the concept of a government limited to securing the unalienable rights of the individual, were said to be outdated and unhistorical. Progress was said to require novel constitutional constructions better adapted to prevailing historical circumstances. More particularly, Progressives generally argued that contemporary circumstances called for greater centralization and rationalization of government, which meant, among other things, its direction by unelected administrative elites more or less immune to the pressure of politics. The Progressive view of government, however, was not confined to specific prescriptions or even general principles but, in line with its overarching philosophy, elastic and flexible. As R. J. Pestritto observed, Progressives championed an evolving conception of government, "one whose ends and scope would change to take on any and all social and economic ills."[1]

Such an expansionist view of legitimate governmental power led Progressives to chafe at the limits on federal power established by the United States Constitution. Federalism, separation of powers, negative rights, and other constitutional restraints on government were said to stand in the way of Progress. Progressives understood, however, that efforts to move beyond the Founders' Constitution would encounter resistance among an American populace historically devoted to both their memory and their principles. They further understood the intimate relation between American political institutions, particularly limited government and the rule of law, and traditional American religious convictions. They well recognized that the American people since the Founding regarded themselves as "endowed by their Creator with certain unalienable rights" and that the Creator in question was generally regarded as the transcendent God of the Bible. The realization of the Progressive aim—the gradual removal of limits on the power of government in the name of greater administrative rationality—thus required simultaneous attack on three pillars of traditional American order—reverence for the Founding Fathers, the U.S. Constitution, and the Christian faith.

Many early Progressives were schooled in the philosophy of American Pragmatism. Pragmatism typically embraces a form of ethical consequentialism, evaluating meaning, truth, or value on the basis of practical consequences and not a priori axioms or principles. Pragmatism, somewhat like Utilitarianism and Socialism, regards right and wrong, good and evil, truth or untruth as determined not by fixed and permanent standards but rather by outcomes, which

---

[1] R. J. Pestritto, *Woodrow Wilson and the Roots of Moaern Liberalism* (Lanham, MD: Rowman & Littlefield Publishers, Inc., 2005).

are necessarily contingent on particular and ever-changing circumstance. The ever-changing circumstances of human history thus lead to changing conceptions of right and wrong. If society is not to be mired in the past, if it is to progress, its moral standards must adapt to the movement of history. On such a view, particular moral conceptions can never be regarded as absolute but only relative to their time and place. Indeed American Progressivism is wedded to a radically relativistic perspective not only with respect to morality but any and all social and cultural phenomena, moral, legal, political, economic, and religious. Progressivism, like its contemporary cousins, Postmodernism and Multiculturalism, challenges the existence of universal, absolute, and immutable Truth that transcends history. On the Progressive view, the only truth accessible to human beings is relative historical truth: what is true in one society or era may or may not be true for other societies shaped by different circumstances or existing in different periods of time. Truth, like every aspect of historical existence, can and does evolve or Progress over time.

On such a view, the allegedly "self-evident Truth" proclaimed in the Declaration of Independence, like the moral Truth proclaimed by Christianity, appear not as absolute but merely relative "truths." Indeed such traditional "truths" appear as little more than quaint historical relics, certainly not binding, universal, and eternal axioms valid for all human beings in all times and places. Progressives acknowledge that the U.S. Constitution may have been culturally appropriate to its time, reflecting widespread beliefs held in an earlier stage of historical development. The same holds true for Christianity and other historical expressions of religious belief. History, however, has moved on and so must morality, religion, law, and government. Thus emerges the

Progressive concept of the "Living Constitution."[2] The clever phrase symbolizes the idea that the U.S. Constitution—the fundamental law and framework of American political order—must be progressively adapted to the forward march of history. To do otherwise, to cling to the outmoded and antiquated eighteenth-century conceptions of the Founders, is to defy the movement of history, to defy Progress. It is to saddle members of contemporary society with the archaic beliefs of a former age and thus preclude a truly representative government "of the people, by the people, for the people." Progress requires movement beyond such putatively historically obsolete conceptions as limited constitutional government, individualism, negative natural rights, free-market capitalism, traditional morality, and justice as the rule of law. Such can only be achieved by throwing off the dead weight of the Founders' Constitution that binds the American people to such obsolete values and institutions. Progress requires a "Living," changing, growing, evolving Constitution, not a petrified and lifeless relic of times long past.

Social Gospel

Progress so conceived further requires movement beyond traditional Christianity. The particularly religious dimension of Progressivism was largely elaborated by its spiritual arm, the Social Gospel movement of the era. Representative leaders included Christian ministers such as Walter Rauschenbusch and Washington Gladden, as well as Richard T. Ely, American economist and founder of the

---

[2] The term originally derives from the title of a 1927 book of the same name by Prof. Howard McBain, while early efforts at developing the concept in modern form have been credited to figures including Oliver Wendell Holmes, Louis D. Brandeis, and Woodrow Wilson.

Christian Social Union.[3] Such Progressive Social-Gospelers assumed the task of revising or adapting Christianity and Judeo-Christian morality to the changing circumstances of history. Many Social Gospel ministers and theologians, like their Progressive counterparts, had received graduate training at contemporary universities in Germany, where they were exposed to the dominant philosophy of the day, so-called German Idealism. Among other teachings, German Idealism held that the "state" (government) possesses an independent reality separate and distinct from the people who compose it. Rauschenbusch and other Social Gospelers would interpret such a concept to mean that society is a "social organism." Progressives such as Woodrow Wilson and others also applied an organic metaphor to society, as reflected in the concept of the "Living" (growing, organic) Constitution.

In all instances, the organic conception of society and government led not only to emphasis on change, evolution, and growth but also elevation of the collective—the putatively organic social whole—over the individual (a mere part). As Arthur Ekirch explains, both Social Gospelers and Progressives were convinced that "[s]ociety in the future would have to be based more and more on an explicit subordination of the individual to a collectivist, or

---

[3] Richard Theodore Ely (1854–1943) was an American economist, author, and leader of the Progressive movement, which called for more government intervention to reform the alleged injustices of capitalism, especially regarding factory conditions, compulsory education, child labor, and labor unions. Ely is best remembered as a founder and the first Secretary of the American Economic Association, as a founder of the Christian Social Union, and as the author of a series of widely-read books on the organized labor movement, socialism, and other social questions.

nationalized, political and social order."[4] Subordination of the individual was regarded as essential to progress and reform. Such a view of course utterly contradicts traditional American conceptions regarding the relation between the individual and government. American social-contract theory conceives society as constituted by individuals endowed with unalienable natural rights and not a living "organism" independent of and superior to the individuals it comprises. The traditional American view presupposes the individual as the exclusive bearer of moral agency and society as a merely nominal abstraction. Moreover, it further regards government ("the state") as a more or less utilitarian organization established by individuals to secure their rights, certainly not an autonomous or self-subsistent entity superior to the people it is meant to serve.

Progressives and Social Gospelers also embraced other aspects of German Idealist philosophy, including the Hegelian philosophy of history.[5] Hegel, like Marx and various other nineteenth-century thinkers, maintained that History is moving by inexorable laws toward a final goal, the "End of History," a path, in Hegel's version, directed by the so-called "cunning of reason."[6] Throughout the autonomous movement of History toward its goal, Hegel further maintained, the highest

---

[4] Arthur Ekirch, *The Decline of American Liberalism* (Oakland, CA: Independent Institute, 2009).

[5] Their experience in Germany led both Progressives and Social Gospelers not only to embrace Idealist philosophy but also its practical application. They particularly admired Bismarck's novel social-welfare policy, which employed government resources to provide guaranteed welfare benefits such as social security and health care to the citizens.

[6] Georg Wilhelm Friedrich Hegel (1770-1831). *Lectures on the Philosophy of History*, originally given as lectures at the University of Berlin in 1821, 1824, 1827, and 1831.

ethical force in society is embodied in government or the state. As Jon Ray explains, for Hegel, "the State is the essential reality and embodies all of human progress. And we are free only when we are all merged into a common will within the State." As Hegel himself put it, the "state" represents nothing less than the "march of God through the World" and "the Divine Idea as it exists on earth." Accordingly, he concludes, "we must . . . worship the State as the manifestation of the Divine on Earth."[7]

Such views stand of course in the starkest possible opposition not only to the traditional Anglo-American conception of government but also the religious conceptions that implicitly inform it. Americans of the founding era certainly did not regard government as "the Divine Idea . . . on earth." On the traditional American view, informed as it is by conventional Judeo-Christian presuppositions, no aspect of the created order is divine. Divinity is an attribute of God alone, and rulers, as Augustine admonished, must remember that they too are men. Indeed to regard the state or government as "divine" is to commit the sin of idolatry.

The efforts of Progressive Social Gospelers to revise or adapt Christianity to the movement of history clearly manifest the radical relativism presupposed by such efforts. Nowhere is such relativism more evident than in their attempt to divinize government or the state in the Hegelian manner.[8] As the Social Gospel minister Washington Gladden put it,

> Let me say . . . that this conception of the state, that it is merely a police force, is, to my mind, a

---

[7] G. W. F. Hegel, *Philosophy of History*, in Jacob Loewenberg, ed, (New York: C. Scribner's Sons, 1929), 388-89, 443-44.

[8] Redivinization is probably the more apt turn, as the modern divinization of the state resembles the pre-Christian or pagan conception that attributed divinity to political rule.

> wholly erroneous conception; . . . *the state is*
> *something far higher and more godlike than this . .*
> *.* [I]f we could only invest it in our thought with
> its true divine character, we should need no
> other agency for the unification of society
> (emphasis added).[9]

In the context of traditional American conceptions of both
government and religion, as well as Gladden's status as a
Christian minister, such a remark is nothing less than
stunning. His comments obviously constitute a veiled
attack on traditional American political principles. The
political thought of the Founders does in fact lead to a view
of government as more or less a "police force," as suggested
by the traditional metaphor of the "night watchman."
They are also utterly incompatible with biblical religion,
however latitudinarian or heterodox. Christianity of course
forbids the imputation of a "true divine character" to
government, or any intramundane entity, but rather
condemned such practice as pagan idolatry from the
outset. Gladden's statement is representative not of
traditional American or Judeo-Christian thought but
rather the modern impulse toward re-divinization or re-
sacralization of the state, the erection, as Nietzsche put it,
of the "New Idol." It represents, not orthodox
Christianity, which radically de-divinized the realm of
government and politics, but rather the corruption of
certain variants of modern Christianity and their
transformation into yet another form of political religion.
Traditional Christianity, again, condemns in no uncertain
terms the attribution of divinity to any aspect of the
created order, precisely the move advanced by Hegel and
Social Gospelers such as Gladden.

---

[9] Cited in Edmund A. Opitz, *The Libertarian Theology of*
Freedom (Tampa: Hallberg Publishing Corporation, 1999), 16-
17. Hereinafter cited as *LTF*.

Such views cannot be reconciled with Christianity, a fact soon apprehended by traditional Christians of the era. The rise of the Social Gospel provoked orthodox American Protestants to reassert the "fundamentals" of Christianity over and against the degenerate socialization of the Christian faith, represented by both the Social Gospel and its fellow traveler, the so-called Christian Socialism that arose in the same period. Such developments, in other words, prompted the rise of what today is known as Christian Fundamentalism. Its early adherents clearly recognized the merely nominal character of the putatively "Christian" Social Gospel.[10] American Social Gospelers and other Progressives thoroughly absorbed the socialistic, and antitheistic, moral vision that rose to prominence in nineteenth-century Europe.

The socialist aspirations of the Social Gospel movement are of course evident in its very name. They are also evident in the attempts of Social Gospel thinkers to reconstruct the image of Christ, indeed, to reconstruct Him in their own image. The era witnessed the publication of various books portraying Jesus Christ as a socialist and asserting the identity of Christian and socialist ethics.[11] As Charles

---

[10] The movement became active in the 1910s after the release of *The Fundamentals*, a ten-volume set of essays, apologetic and polemic, written by conservative Protestant theologians to defend what they regarded as Protestant orthodoxy.

[11] For instance, *In His Steps* (1897) and *The Reformer* (1902), by the Congregational minister Charles Sheldon, who coined the motto "What would Jesus do?" In his personal life, Sheldon was committed to Christian Socialism and identified strongly with the Social Gospel movement. Walter Rauschenbusch, one of the leading early theologians of the Social Gospel in the United States, indicated that his theology had been inspired by Sheldon's novels. In 1892, Rauschenbusch and several other leading writers and advocates of the Social Gospel formed a group called the Brotherhood of the Kingdom. Members of this group produced many of the written works that defined the

Cashdollar explains in *The Transformation of Theology, 1830-1890,* Christianity in the nineteenth century found itself in a kind of dialectical confrontation with the novel socialist morality of the era. Socialism portrayed itself as a decided moral advance over traditional Christianity, which was relentlessly criticized and condemned for its allegedly selfish individualism and egoism. Christianity was bluntly condemned as the Religion of the Selfish.[12] Socialism, by contrast, was said to embody altruistic concern for others, for all human beings, not merely the individual or particular privileged groups. Certain Christian denominations accepted and assimilated the socialist critique of Christianity. Rather than defending their faith against such charges, they embraced the views of their critics, often becoming as socialist as the Socialists. Such assimilation is of course explicit in those denominations that embraced the Social Gospel, but prevailing trends influenced other Christian denominations as well. Christ himself was reinvented as a socialist and socialism held to be the true expression of Christian spirituality and ethics. The transcendent core of Christian faith was eviscerated or obscured, and spiritual aspirations redirected toward amelioration of material suffering in this world. The Kingdom of God was no longer conceived as "within" or beyond, as in orthodox Christian theology, but more or less identified with this world—the earthly or temporal realm of society, government, and material concerns.

---

theology of the Social Gospel movement and gave it public prominence. These included Rauschenbusch's *Christianity and the Social Crisis* (1907) and *Christianizing the Social Order* (1912), as well as Batten's *The New Citizen*ship (1898) and *The Social Task of Christianity* (1911).

[12] ". . . Christianity gives to morality an essentially selfish character. . . ." J.S. Mill, *On Liberty and Other Writings*, ed, Stefan Collini (Cambridge: Cambridge University Press, 1995 [1859]), 51.

Such conceptions resemble the similar exchange of "vertical" for "horizontal" transcendence embodied in the modern ideological movements. The Social Gospel movement was in the forefront of such efforts in the American context. The movement was a uniquely American expression of the existential drive that Eric Voegelin associates with modernity more generally, that is, the futile attempt to "immanentize the Eschaton." The Social Gospel, like the more virulent ideological movements, collapsed the tension between the transcendent and immanent dimensions of existence, attempting instead to materialize the Kingdom of God within history. The transcendent pole of human of experience was obscured and spiritual aspirations, traditionally oriented toward a transcendent God beyond time and history, redirected to exclusively worldly or mundane concerns.[13]   Social Gospelers replaced the traditional transcendent orientation of the Christian faith not with the promised land of the Marxian vision—ideal communism—but rather various forms of immanent or this-worldly "social" ministry—food kitchens, medical uplift, education, and other forms of material welfare. Presbyterians, Congregationalists, Methodists, Northern Baptists and other denominations influenced by the Social Gospel developed various "social creeds" that emphasized the "social" significance of the Gospel. By 1912 eleven denominations pledged to carry out "social service" programs.

While such charitable assistance has long been regarded as a Christian obligation, the Social Gospelers moved far beyond traditional Christian concern for the less fortunate. An essential feature of the Social Gospel was its truncation of religious obligation to provision of mundane social

---

[13] See Linda C. Raeder, "Voegelin on Gnosticism, Modernity, and the Balance of Consciousness" (*Political Science Reviewer*, Vol. XXXVI, 2007).

welfare, typically of a material nature. Religious obligation was more or less reduced to intraworldly "service to Humanity"; traditional obligation to serve the transcendent God more or less faded from view. As Albrecht Ritschl explained, salvation, according to the new Social Gospel, "was not to be interpreted in terms of a future life, but in terms of service in a this-worldly kingdom of human goodness."[14] As Woodrow Wilson propounded the Humanistic social creed, "There is no higher religion than human service. To work for the common good is the greatest creed."[15] Wilson followed in the footsteps of earlier prophets of the Humanist evangel, such as J.S. Mill. Mill had decades earlier proclaimed the moral superiority of the Religion of Humanity to orthodox Christianity and "service to Humanity . . . the law of our lives." In all such constructs, the traditional Christian obligation to serve one's fellows in service to God, conceived as a triangular relation among God, the individual, and his fellow human beings, is replaced by a dualistic Service to Humanity, a relation forged solely between human beings. The third, most crucial, leg of the orthodox Christian conception—God, the Source of the Christian obligation to serve other human beings—more or less disappears from view. God, as Nietzsche had pointed out, is dead.

Social Gospelers shared with communist true believers not only an ultimate aim—the creation of the Kingdom of God on earth—but also mutual belief in the perfectibility of man by means of "social" change. From a strictly theological perspective, the Social Gospel and similar quasi-religious movements within modern and postmodern society, such as so-called Liberation Theology, represent a corruption and degeneration of Christianity. Their chief significance for modern political

---

[14] Albrecht Ritschl, cited in Opitz, *LTF*, 16.
[15] Woodrow Wilson (December 28, 1856 - February 03, 1924).

developments is the fact that all such movements were (and are) eager to employ the coercive force of government to achieve their ends, whether such are regarded as the will of History or the will of God. Various Social Gospelers, for instance, advocated governmental redistribution of wealth in the name of social justice, said to be an application of the "teachings of Jesus" and the "law of love."[16] Others advocated outright socialism, including government ownership of significant resources such as land, water supply, mines, and so on.

Such proposals cannot be defended on traditional Christian grounds let alone said to follow from Christian teaching. Neither socialism proper nor political redistribution of wealth can be morally justified on the grounds of traditional Christian ethics. Such forms of economic organization and policy are strictly prohibited not only by the longstanding Judeo-Christian validation of the rule of law in general but the right to property in particular. As previously observed, the moral legitimacy of private property is established and presupposed by the absolute biblical injunction against theft. The prohibition against taking a person's property without his consent rules out the moral legitimacy of both socialism proper and political redistribution of wealth, neither of which can be achieved without taking someone's property without consent. The only way to avoid such a conclusion is the improbable if not impossible achievement of universal voluntary consent to any proposed policy involving political distribution or redistribution of wealth.

The radical relativism of the Social Gospelers, like that of their Progressive counterparts, however, did provide a way around such moral obstacles. The Progressives, as said, denied the validity of moral absolutes, Christian or otherwise. The Social Gospelers were Progressives. Accordingly, they denied the absolutely binding nature of

---

[16] Opitz, *LTF*, 18.

the Judeo-Christian Decalogue. Historical criticism undertaken in the previous century, they argued, had made several important discoveries that undermined the moral authority of the Ten Commandments. Not only had such research uncovered the "fact," previously noted, that Jesus was a social reformer or even an outright socialist but also that certain of the Commandments served a suspect, even nefarious, purpose, namely, protecting the "haves" against the "have-nots." On the basis of such putative discovery, Social Gospelers and Progressives concluded that the Judeo-Christian prohibition of stealing must not be regarded as absolutely but only relatively or conditionally binding on the human conscience. Morality, as every other historical entity, must be regarded not as fixed and unalterable but rather evolving and progressing. In this instance, Progress requires the present age to advance beyond the self-serving interpretation placed upon the Ten Commandments in former centuries. The Decalogue must not be regarded as a set of absolute injunctions transcending time and space but rather relative moral rules whose significance and meaning vary (progress) over the course of history. Such a weakening of moral absolutes was widely embraced not only by Social Gospelers and Progressives but other Christian denominations influenced by their teaching as well.[17]

Proponents of the Social Gospel shared with their Marxist brethren not only the demand for political redistribution of wealth and even outright socialization of various resources but a deeper substratum of belief as well. At the core of both systems of thought lies a shared belief in *determinism*. Philosophical determinism has been formally defined as a "theory that all events, including moral choices, are completely determined by previously existing

---

[17]See, for example, *The Book of Resolutions of the United Methodist Church 2016* (Nashville: Cokesbury, 2016).

causes. . . [such] that humans cannot act otherwise than they do."[18] In other words, determinism is a broad and general category of philosophical thought encompassing various particular theories united by a defining attribute, namely, the belief that something other than free choice "determines" or "causes" individual experience. Modern determinism takes many forms, from the economic and historical determinism of Marx to the psychological determinism of Sigmund Freud to the genetic or biological determinism of contemporary science.

Karl Marx taught that prevailing economic relations in a society "determine" the consciousness and behavior of its members. Social Gospelers extended such determinism beyond the realm of economics per se to the social environment more generally. The environment of the individual, and not the individual himself, was said to determine his behavior. Determinism so conceived, conventionally if not surprisingly referred to as environmental or social determinism, is yet another distinguishing feature of the Social Gospel and one that further turns orthodox Christianity on its head. Traditional Christianity, as previously discussed, regards the battle between good and evil as occurring within the heart and soul of the individual, the locus of moral agency, freedom, and responsibility. The character of any given society, including both its characteristic social, political, and economic institutions and prevailing social conditions, manifests the character of the individuals who constitute it. The social "environment" is regarded not as "cause" of human experience but rather its "effect," the manifestation of the values, beliefs, and actions of the individuals who constitute society. Christianity, moreover, does not permit individuals to blame external or environmental conditions for their values, beliefs, actions, or experience. Eve's decision to eat the fruit could not be blamed on the serpent

---

[18] Encyclopedia Britannica, 2016.

or apple tree. Her action was determined not by her environment—the existence of the serpent and tree—but rather individual choice, the exercise of free will. Both the priority of individual values to social conditions and the existence of free will lead to the conclusion that improvement of the "social environment" necessarily requires preliminary improvement of the individuals who shape it. No magic, political or otherwise, can create a good society out of bad people.

Modern Western determinism rose to prominence in the wake of the "death of God." One of the central elements of the biblical worldview is of course the conviction that human beings, made in the image of God, are endowed with free will, the capacity for voluntary choice. If God is dead, however, then so is the conception of individual free will. Indeed the existence of free will was a significant and much debated issue in nineteenth-century England, the period that witnessed both militant hostility toward Christianity and the accompanying rise of antitheistic social morality. So-called Christian Voluntarists of the era countered the arguments of anti-theological thinkers by pointing precisely to the existence of free will as definitive "proof" of the existence of God.[19] Such efforts would prove more or less in vain. The social success of the antitheistic forces led not only to evisceration of Christianity but its characteristic conception of free will as well. Determinism emerged to fill the void.

Accordingly, various modern determinists, from Rousseau to Marx to the Social Gospelers, reject the traditional view that conceives the social environment as reflecting prior individual values, belief, and practice, dependent as it is on the concept of free will. Evil is said to

---

[19] J.S. Mill, *An Examination of Sir William Hamilton's Philosophy*, vol. 9, *Collected Works of John Stuart Mill*, 33 vols, ed, John M. Robson, intro Alan Ryan (Toronto: University of Toronto Press, 1979). Hereinafter cited as *CW*.

result not from individual moral choice, regarded as yet another illusion of the Judeo-Christian imagination, but rather the external social environment and/or faulty social institutions of one sort or another. Rousseau attributed the source of evil to the *ancien regime* and its institutions, Marx to the capitalist economic system. The Social Gospelers attributed it to the social environment. Moreover, just as the elimination of the evils perceived by Rousseau required transformation of existing French institutions and the evils perceived by Marx required transformation of the economic system, so the evils perceived by the Social Gospelers required transformation of the social environment. The elimination of evil and creation of a good society require not the transformation, conversion, or moral development of its individual members but rather reconstruction of the social environment believed to engender bad or vicious behavior. As Rev. Irving E. Howard summarized the Social Gospel view, "[i]nstead of the converted individual changing the environment, a changed environment was supposed to change the individual."[20]

The social or environmental determinism of the Social Gospelers took an ominous turn when conjoined with a belief acquired from their Progressive brethren, namely, that requisite change of the social environment could be achieved through judicious employment of the coercive power of government ("social engineering"). In 1885, Gladden attended a conference at which he was introduced to the idea of "using the force of the state to achieve . . . social righteousness. . . ."[21] Arch-Progressive Woodrow Wilson was in attendance at the conference, as was Richard T. Ely, the aforementioned Progressive economist who championed greater governmental intervention in economic and social life. Upon embracing the (anti-

---

[20] Opitz, *LTF*, 12.
[21] Ibid., 13.

Augustinian) belief in the efficacy of coercive force with respect to moral reform, Social Gospelers joined hands with Progressives in a mutual effort to remove constitutional limits on the power of the federal government. The Progressives regarded such limits as obstacles to Progress; the Social Gospelers came to regard them as obstacles to establishing the Kingdom of God on earth. The achievement of the Kingdom thus required a reinterpretation not only of Christianity but also the U.S. Constitution. Progressives and Social Gospelers marched in step toward achievement of their mutual goals.

Proponents of the Social Gospel also united with Progressive and socialist fellow travelers in attacking capitalism. Marx's assault on the liberal economic order involved a frontal assault not only on capitalism but also its corollary religious traditions. Marx not only confessed his "hatred of the gods" but dismissed religion as the "opium of the people," an illusory and ultimately poisonous means of escaping the sufferings of this world.[22] The Social Gospelers, by contrast, did not advocate outright rejection of Christianity but rather its reinterpretation and identification with socialism. In 1889, the Society of Christian Socialists was formed in Boston to "show that the aim of socialism is embraced in the aim of Christianity." In the same year, Gladden spoke on the topic of "Christian socialism" at a council of Congregational churches. Although Gladden did not

---

[22] The full quote from Karl Marx has been translated as follows: "Religion is the sigh of the oppressed creature, the heart of a heartless world, and the soul of soulless conditions. It is the opium of the people." The quotation originates from the introduction of Marx's proposed work "A Contribution to the Critique of Hegel's Philosophy of Right." The "Contribution" was never completed but Marx published the introduction (written in 1843) in his own journal, *Deutsch-Französische Jahrbüch*er.

identify himself as a full-fledged socialist, he shared its denigration of individualism, which he, like his socialist brethren, linked to the market order. As Gladden put it, "It begins to be clear that Christianity is not individualism. The Christian has encountered no deadlier foe during the last century than that individualistic philosophy which underlies the competitive system." Other Social Gospel ministers agreed: "Business itself today is wrong . . . based on competitive strife for profits. But this is the exact opposite of Christianity. We must change the system. . . ."[23] Rauschenbusch attacked both competition and business monopoly. In 1934 the Congregational-Christian churches established a Council for Social Action that summed up the anti-capitalist aspirations of the Social Gospel movement.

> [The Council resolved to work toward] . . . the abolition of the system responsible for these destructive elements in our common life [the competitive market system], by eliminating the system's incentives and habits, the legal forms which sustain it, and the moral ideals which justify it. The inauguration of a genuinely cooperative social economy democratically planned to adjust production to consumption requirements, to modify or eliminate private ownership of the means of production or distribution wherever such ownership interferes with the social good.[24]

The conclusion of Rev. Howard is to the point— "the Social Gospel as it developed in American Protestantism was not an application of the teachings of Jesus."[25] It

---

[23] Cited in Opitz, *LTF*, 14.

[24] Ibid., 20.

[25] Ibid.10

represents, on the contrary, yet another manifestation of the tremendous "shift in faith" that took place in Western society during the modern period. Voegelin characterizes such a shift as the general eclipse of transcendence. Rev. Howard further specifies the characteristically modern dynamic as a shift "from God to man, from eternity to time, from the individual to the [collective] group, individual conversion to social coercion, . . . from the church to the state," and, not least, from individual spiritual freedom to social determinism.[26] Such are among the consequences of the "death of God" in its American expression.

Secular Messianism and the Social Religion

The Social Gospelers, like many self-described Christian socialists and Christian altruists to the present day, seemed unaware of the nature of the social creed they absorbed from Europe, including both its origin as an explicit rival to traditional Christianity and its fundamental incompatibility with biblical faith. Christianity and socialism cannot be reconciled. The Social Gospelers, as discussed, could only appear to do so by revising Christianity in certain fundamental ways, for instance, reinventing Jesus as a social reformer and relativizing the Ten Commandments so that they no longer represent absolute and universal moral prohibitions. As important, however, the Social Gospelers and their descendants among the so-called Christian Left seem oblivious to the profane and profoundly anti-Christian roots of the social morality they came to attribute to Christianity itself. The social religion and morality of the nineteenth century, later championed by the Social Gospel, was deliberately constructed as a rival to, and substitute for, orthodox Christianity and traditional biblical morality. The Social

[26] Ibid., 11.

Gospel was an important carrier of the profoundly anti-Christian morality championed by socialists, Marxists, Positivists, and other representatives of the antitheistic impulse in the eighteenth and nineteenth centuries. The profane and anti-Christian roots of the novel social morality constructed in the era are clearly evidenced by the historical record.[27]

Ethical and social thought in the West is generally thought to have undergone a gradual process of secularization throughout the course of the eighteenth and nineteenth centuries. The term "secularization," however, is often employed carelessly, and, as Jacob Viner observed, "is liable to deceive." Viner himself defines secularization as a "lessening of the influence . . . of ecclesiastical authority and traditional church creeds, and a shifting of weight from dogma and revelation and other-worldliness to reason and sentiment and considerations of temporal welfare."[28] Viner's definition, however, is itself somewhat misleading. The notion that secularization represents a "lessening" of the influence of religious authority, creeds and the like fails to capture the essence of such change. The weakening of Western religious belief did not result from a more or less autonomous process of social change but was rather impelled by militant activists determined to undermine, if not eradicate, the traditional theological orientation of the West and the social and political order it sustained. The aim of such activists, as James Crimmins

---

[27] Linda C. Raeder, *John Stuart Mill and the Religion of Humanity* (Columbia, MO: University of Missouri Press, 2002), hereinafter cited as *Religion of Humanity*.

[28] Jacob Viner, *The Role of Providence in the Social Order: An Essay in Intellectual History* (Princeton: Princeton University Press, 2015), 55.

observes, was to "extirpat[e] religious beliefs, even the idea of religion itself from the minds of men."[29]

The "death of God" enacted throughout the nineteenth century was characterized by an aggressive and even militant anti-theological thrust. Marx was an important leader of the modern "revolt against God" but far from alone in that endeavor. Prodigious efforts were made throughout the nineteenth century not only to undermine the religious traditions of the West, in particular, Christianity, but also to establish one form or another of secular, social, or political religion to serve as its replacement. Marxism was not the only political religion developed during the period. Various fellow travelers also aimed to capture the spiritual energy traditionally channeled toward a transcendent God and personal salvation and reorient it toward the promise of collective salvation through secular and ultimately political pursuits. The propagation of such intramundane secular creeds, including Benthamite Utilitarianism and the previously mentioned Religion of Humanity, was infused with intense spiritual energy. Their founders and carriers invested such constructs with ultimate, and salvific, value, both regarding and experiencing their constructed "religions without a God" as full-fledged religion, a fact expressly acknowledged by their devotees.[30] In his *Autobiography*, for instance, J. S. Mill describes his conversion to Benthamite utilitarianism, which Bentham

---

[29] Jeremy Bentham: "A new religion would be an odd sort of thing without a name—[I] propose . . . Utilitarianism." Cited in Mary Warnock, introduction, J.S. Mill, *Utilitarianism, On Liberty, Essay on Bentham* (Cleveland: World Publishing, 1962), 9.

[30] Richard H. Crossman, *The God That Failed*. New York: Columbia University Press (2001).

himself called "a new religion," as an experience that struck him with all the force of religious conversion.[31]

The roots of the quasi-Christian morality of the Social Gospel and American Progressivism can be traced to eighteenth-century France, especially the thought of Henri de Saint-Simon and his followers, the St. Simonians and Auguste Comte. St. Simon and Comte were two of the more influential of the various secular messiahs to emerge in the modern and postmodern world.[32] Neither social savior made a secret of their mutual aim: to usher in a new world defined in opposition to preceding stages of human intellectual and social history, the so-called "theological" and "metaphysical" stages of the human mind.[33] The terminology varied—St. Simon would have his "terrestrial . . . New Christianity," Comte his "Positive Religion" or "Religion of Humanity"—-but the aspiration was identical in all cases. All the secular religions formulated by the French messiahs were variations on the same theme. As Frank Manuel put it, they all "represented . . . a deflection of love from the God of the Christians to mankind and a transfer of interest from the future of the immortal soul to man's destiny on earth."[34] They all preached the by-now-familiar gospel of social and political salvation to be achieved here and now, in this world.

---

[31] Mill, *Autobiography and Literary Essays,* vol 1, *CW,* ed, 1981, 68.

[32] Cf. de Lubac, *Drama*; Frank E. Manuel, *The New World of Henri Saint-Simon* (Cambridge: Harvard University Press, 1956); D.C. Charlton, *Secular Religions in France 1815-1870* (London: Oxford University Press, 1963); Eric Voegelin, *From Enlightenment to Revolution*, ed, John D. Hallowell (Durham: Duke University Press, 1975); Jacob Talmon, *Political Messianism* (NY: Frederick A. Praeger, 1960).

[33] Manuel, *The New World of Henri Saint-Simon,* 123.

[34] Ibid.

The various new secular religions were invariably accompanied by newly formulated moralities— "terrestrial," "positive," "social," "purely human"— intended to replace the "theological" morality bound up with mankind's earlier and now putatively obsolete stage of development. The secular messiahs thus pursued two related aims. First, spiritual aspirations were to be reoriented away from the traditional transcendent God and toward a worldly, mundane substitute of one kind or another. The proposed replacement for God assumed various forms—Comte's "Great Being" of Humanity, the Social Gospelers' "Kingdom of God" on earth; the communist paradise that was the End of History, and so on. All such constructs, however, share an essential and defining attribute, that is, they all relocate the ultimate object of religious devotion and obligation from God to Man. The second and related aim was the social establishment of a new religion that embodied the new "terrestrial" spirituality and morality. Indeed, certain of the secular messiahs were driven by even more grandiose ambition—to secure the final eradication of theology and metaphysics and all such transcendent orientation implied for human existence.[35] The realization of the secular messiahs' mission, then, required both the establishment of a secular or intraworldly religion and simultaneous replacement of theologically grounded morality with a naturalistic substitute constructed not by God but rather man. It further required the reorientation of religious aspirations and sentiments away from otherworldly

---

[35] According to James Crimmins, Jeremy Bentham's aim was nothing less than "to extirpat[e] religious beliefs, even the idea of religion itself from the minds of men." James Crimmins, "Religion, Utility, and Politics: Bentham vs. Paley," in *Religion, Secularization, and Political Thought: Thomas Hobbes to J.S. Mill* (London: Routledge, 1990), 140.

concerns toward those, as Mill said, "confined to the limits of the earth."[36]

The social morality preached by the Social Gospelers, American Progressives, and the Christian Left more generally ultimately derives from such efforts. The morality of altruism and Service to Humanity is not of Christian inspiration but rather the opposite—a construction deliberately devised to replace, and improve upon, traditional Judeo-Christian ethics. In order to facilitate its acceptance, moreover, the novel anti-theological or "purely human" morality was further and deliberately devised to resemble traditional ethics. The St. Simonians, for instance, well understood that most members of eighteenth- and nineteenth-century European society regarded themselves as Christian. Not only would they have resisted overt attacks on Christianity but, in the English context, Christianity was protected against public criticism by various laws prohibiting blasphemy. Efforts to undermine Christianity were thus often conducted in a surreptitious and manipulative manner. St. Simon for instance, cunningly developed the strategy of employing traditional Christian symbolism and sentiment and investing it with novel social and political meaning. Christian symbols were reinterpreted and manipulated in the hope that unsuspecting believers might thus be more easily persuaded to embrace the new naturalistic and humanistic (antitheistic) creed. J. S. Mill, a fellow traveler with the St. Simonians in this regard as in others, similarly employed traditional Christian symbolism, including the person of Christ, to advance the anti-Christian Religion of Humanity, the proximate source of contemporary Secular Humanism.

---

[36] J.S. Mill, "Utility of Religion," *Collected Works of John Stuart Mill*, (Toronto: University of Toronto Press, 1972), Vol. 10: 421. Hereinafter cited as *CW*.

The St. Simonians and other secular messiahs of the era were acutely aware that religion provides the essential bond and animating force of human society. The "critical philosophy" of the eighteenth century, they believed, had successfully undermined Christianity, a task they regarded as necessary and on the whole salutary. Such an achievement, however, only realized half of the historical mission. What remained was the articulation and propagation of a new creed, a new faith, a new and "higher" religion to replace Christianity, which perhaps had been suitable in former ages but was no longer in harmony with the presently advanced state of the human mind. As Mill expressed the common sentiment of the secular messiahs, "Christianity . . . is gone, never to return, only what was best in it to reappear in another, and still higher form. . . ."[37] Progress required the development or purification of Christianity. To that end, the St. Simonians proposed the "New Christianity" or "Religion of Love" developed by their leader. As St. Simon explains in *Nouveau Christianisme:*

> . . . God has related everything to a single principle, and deduced everything from a single principle. . . . Now, according to this principle given to men by God as a guide for their conduct, they should organize their community in the way which will be most advantageous to the greatest number; they should make it their aim in all their undertakings and actions, to promote as quickly and completely as possible the moral and physical welfare of the most numerous class. *I maintain that in that, and that alone, consists the divine part of the Christian religion.* . . . God has given to men a single principle. . . . He has ordered men to organize

---

[37] Mill to Carlyle, October 5, 1833, *CW* 12: 180-182.

their community in such a way as to secure for
the poorest class the quickest and most complete
improvement of their moral and physical
condition . . . . (emphasis added)

Christianity in the hands St. Simon is reduced to political
and economic ideology, more or less the Utilitarian
principle of the Greatest Happiness of the Greatest
Number. It becomes nothing more than a tool of politics,
exclusively concerned with social organization and
material welfare. Salvation is reinterpreted as political or
collective salvation to be attained through political and
economic action; the spiritual and transcendent dimension
of biblical religion disappears from view. St. Simon is the
father not only of Christian Socialism and the Social
Gospel but all modern religious movements that reduce
religious obligation to the amelioration of human suffering
in this world. Marxist Liberation Theology and its cousin,
Black Liberation Theology, are characteristic, as are certain
forms of Christian advocacy for "social justice."

The essence of the "New Christianity" is its resolutely
this-worldly character, its attempt to reinvent Christianity
by eviscerating its transcendent orientation. Such an effort
necessarily involved the reconstruction of biblical morality.
Traditional Judeo-Christian morality is of course rooted in
a transcendent Ground of Being, a divine Source beyond
this world. Such is precisely the aspect of traditional
morality—its transcendent or theological source—that
must be eliminated if the goals of the secular messiahs were
to be realized. St. Simon thus attacks traditional biblical
morality as mere "celestial ethics" that must be replaced by
"terrestrial ethics." Comte's version proposes the novel
morality of "altruism" as the naturalistic moral standard to
accompany the Positivist Religion of the Future.
Bentham's version proposes the standard of nontheological
utilitarianism. His acolyte, J.S. Mill, castigates "theological
morality" as inferior to the "purely human" morality

embodied in both his version of utilitarianism and the Religion of Humanity he intended to substitute for the "baseless fancies" of traditional religion.[38] Marx stridently proclaims man as the highest divinity, the author of right and wrong.

The Law of the Three Stages

A brief discussion of the underlying philosophy of history embraced by the French secular messiahs will further clarify their goals and methods, as well as their significance for subsequent American developments. One of the characteristic developments of the nineteenth century was the production of various comprehensive philosophies of history. Authors such as Comte, Hegel, Marx, and others believed they had gained insight into the inexorable laws said to govern the overarching course of human history. History, it was claimed, possesses an immutable pattern, typically consisting of three stages leading toward a final goal or end. Voegelin attributes the source of such symbolism to the writings of the twelve-century monk, Joachim of Flora. The Marxist variant divided history into three phases, slavery, feudalism, and capitalism. Hegel also divided history into three stages, based on the degree of freedom achieved in various epochs (periods in which one was free, many were free, all were free).[39] The St. Simonian and Comtean versions had a different emphasis. As John Eckalbar explains,

---

[38] J.S. Mill, "Utility of Religion," in *CW* 10: 420.

[39] For Hegel, the widest view of history reveals three most important stages of development: Oriental imperial (the stage of oneness, of suppression of freedom), Greek social democracy (the stage of expansion, in which some but not all were free, and Christian constitutional monarchy (which represents the reintegration of freedom in constitutional government (all are free).

> [The St. Simonians] drew a parallel between the growth of mankind in history and the growth of a human body. Both mankind and the body were said to develop from stage to stage by the 'law of progressive development'. Humanity . . . is a collective entity. This entity has grown from generation to generation as a man grows in the course of years, according to its own physical law, which has been one of progressive development. The human race 'grows progressively according to invariable laws'. . . . The 'law of the perfectibility of the human species' is key to understanding history. By the law of perfectibility, it is ordained that mankind pass from the miseries of savagery to the bliss of a secular paradise.[40]

In the progress toward secular perfection, according to the St. Simonians, political society passes through two alternating modes of historical existence—"organic epochs" and "critical epochs." Two "organic epochs" have previously appeared in history. The first was the period of Greek and Roman polytheism ending with Socrates in Greece and Augustus in Rome; the second began with the preaching of the Gospels and ended with Martin Luther. The first "organic" epoch was followed by the "critical" epoch of philosophy, during which polytheism was undermined by the classical philosophers. The close of the second "organic" epoch came with the Protestant Reformation. The second "critical" epoch would come to a close upon the rise of the new era of secular perfectibility proclaimed by Saint-Simon and preached by his disciples. The *Doctrine* was written to announce that "the times have

---

[40] John C. Eckalbar, "The Saint-Simonian Philosophy of History: A Note." *History and Theory* © 1977.

been fulfilled and the hour about to strike when, according to the Saint-Simonian transformation of the Christian word, "all shall be called and all shall be chosen."[41] The Saint Simonians regarded themselves as heralds of the third and final "organic" epoch. As Saint-Simon said, "the transition which is now taking place . . . consists in the passage from the theological system to the terrestrial and positive system."[42] As we have seen, such passage is the defining attribute of St. Simon's "New Christianity"—the replacement of "celestial" with "terrestrial" Christianity, conceived as an intraworldly program of positivist social and political reform. Voegelin's "immanentization of the eschaton" is inevitably brought to mind.

Comte's version of a philosophy of history embodies the identical move. He also asserted the existence of an inexorable law of history, the so-called "law of three stages"—theological, metaphysical, and positivist. Comte's law of history, like Saint-Simon's, is identified with "laws of progressive development," more particularly, with laws governing the development of the human mind and especially its capacity for abstraction and generalization. According to Comte, the progressive development of man's mental capacity is reflected in humanity's evolving conceptions of God. Early growth in the capacity for abstraction and generalization enabled human beings to move beyond the most primitive stage, polytheism, in which the government of nature was attributed to many minds (gods), a stage Comte labels the "theological" stage of the mind. Further growth in the capacity for generalization led eventually to the recognition that nature is governed by one mind (god); monotheism is thus characteristic of what Comte calls the "metaphysical stage" of the mind. At this stage, however, the growth of the human mind is not yet complete. Comte anticipates

---

[41] Eckalbar, ibid.
[42] Saint-Simon, cited in Manuel, ibid. 227.

yet further mental development that will culminate in the final stage of the human mind and history, the so-called "positivist" stage. This third and final stage, unlike earlier stages, is based on true and final knowledge of the source of the government of nature. Final knowledge discloses that the actual source is not God but rather invariable law embodied in modern science. At this final stage, the human mind has developed to the point where it recognizes that the phenomena of nature are governed, not by divine agency, whether of many gods or one god, but rather by the invariable and impersonal laws of positive science. The final goal of history is thus identical for St. Simon and Comte—a post-theological, post-Christian society free from the theological and metaphysical superstitions that prevailed in earlier stages of human development. Progress, in both cases, involves movement beyond transcendent religion.

The St. Simonian and Comtean "laws of progressive development" are clearly an important source of later American Progressivism. For St. Simon, Comte, and the Progressives, Progress entails the movement from theology and metaphysics to post-theological or naturalistic positivism. In other words, Progress so conceived entails the ongoing demise of the traditional religious faith of the West, defined by its orientation toward a transcendent God. Such a conception of Progress also confirms the merely relative or provisional nature of all social institutions. All institutions, religious, moral, political, legal, and economic, are conceived as fluid constructs continually adapting to time and change. Every such change is further regarded as superior to that which it supplants, insuring that history "progresses" or advances toward the ever-greater perfection of human society. Paradoxically, such a conception, which identifies Progress with movement through time, simultaneously points to a final goal of one kind or another, an end to time and change, the End of History.

The most crucial element of the conception of Progress advanced by the St. Simonians, Comte, and their Progressive descendants, however, is the assertion that Progress necessarily entails the ongoing decline of the traditional religious framework of Western civilization. Such thinkers concede that earlier stages of human development, the polytheistic and monotheistic stages, were valuable and necessary within their own historic contexts. Such was especially true of the monotheistic phase, particularly its medieval expression (Christendom). The beliefs and institutional manifestations of monotheism, however, cannot be regarded as eternal and absolute truth but only provisional stages on the road to the final stage of human development—post-theological positivism or "science." Elements of Christianity might be preserved in the final age, provided Christianity is "purified" or "improved" in line with the advanced state of knowledge that has been attained by human progress. The secular messiahs believed that they were poised on the threshold of a new era; the final stage of history was at hand. Indeed the nineteenth century was permeated with the expectation of imminent transformation, whether to the final stage of communism, as in Marx, or the final stage of post-theological positivism, as in St. Simon, Comte, and fellow travelers such as Mill. Such a sense partially accounts for the urgency with which they constructed the alternative religions intended to fill the spiritual void that ensued upon the "death of God."

Secular Humanism: The Religion of Humanity

The philosophies of history developed in the nineteenth century, whether of Comtean, Marxian, or Hegelian inspiration, generally share the assumption that Progess necessarily entails the elimination of faith in a transcendent Source beyond history. American Progressivism inherited such a belief and carried it forward in the American context, with effects that continue to the present day. Such influence is evident, for instance, in the rise in the United States of so-called Secular Humanism, the moral arm of modern-liberal Progressivism. Both trends, Progressivism and secular humanism, are of considerable importance for modern American developments, in particular, their mutual relation to the anti-theological considerations under discussion. We have discussed the relation of Progressivism to the speculation of thinkers such as St. Simon and Comte. Secular humanism emerges from the same spring. A closer examination of the Religion of Humanity, the proximate forebear of contemporary secular humanism, will serve to further illustrate the process whereby positivist and Progressivist assumptions were assimilated by Anglo-American consciousness, in particular, the manner in which Christianity was reconstructed and incorporated into the movement of Progress toward final immanent perfection.

We have discussed the confrontation between nineteenth-century Christianity and the new social ethics. The antitheistic social morality championed by Marx and other secular messiahs was portrayed as superior to traditional Judeo-Christian ethics and the free society it sustained. Traditional morality, the personal morality of the Bible, was condemned as individualistic, egoistic, and selfish, allegedly concerned only with the individual's personal salvation and not, like socialism, with the good of the whole. The novel social morality was championed not only by outright socialists and communists such as Marx, but also fellow travelers such as St. Simon, Comte, Mill, and others. The new Socialist Man would willingly serve the collective good of society; Comte's man of the future would similarly "Live for Others," as the slogan of the Positivist Religion of Humanity later put it. The virtue of altruism, associated with the Positivist faith, was juxtaposed to its opposite, the vice of egoism, associated with Christianity.

Straightforward Marxism was undoubtedly too rich a brew for American consumption, advocating as it did outright rejection of traditional religion ("the opium of the people"). The New Christianity and Religion of Humanity advanced by the French messiahs, however, would prove more palatable to American tastes. By the turn of the twentieth century, the period that also witnessed the rise of Progressivism and the Social Gospel, such quasi-religious constructs had achieved a measure of social success in both England and America. Temples to Humanity checkered the New England landscape, and positivist ethical injunctions such as "service to Humanity" were trumpeted from on high by persons no less influential than Woodrow Wilson. Over time, the aspirations embodied in the Religion of Humanity and similar intramundane spiritual constructs were widely assimilated by Anglo-American consciousness. Morality was transformed away from the personal and individual and toward the "social"—the "altruistic" and "terrestrial" morality first championed by the St. Simonians. The Social Gospel movement is characteristic. Indeed, as we have seen, the triumph of the nineteenth-century social ideal eventually led to conflation of the moral and social. F. A. Hayek has enumerated over a hundred different uses in modern ethical and political discourse of what he calls the "weasel word" ("social").[43] Everyone is familiar, for instance, with such concepts as social justice, social conscience, social responsibility, social morality, social democracy, social problems, social work, social service, and so on. Consequentialist "social" aims are widely regarded

---

[43] F.A. Hayek, *The Fatal Conceit: The Errors of Socialism* (Chicago: University of Chicago Press, 1991), 114-117. The usage of the adjective 'social' obscures rather than clarifies the meaning of the word it qualifies, casting a fog over the legitimate or traditional meaning attached to concepts central to Western and American moral and political discourse.

as self-evidently good. Indeed in many quarters social concerns have supplanted traditional morality, the biblically based personal morality that shaped the development of Western liberal society.

Millions of persons over the course of the past century were persuaded of the inferiority of traditional biblical ethics to socialist ethics, a conviction still passionately embraced by many members of contemporary society. The vast majority, certainly within Anglo-American society, did not absorb such a conviction directly from Marx but rather through other more culturally persuasive sources. Anglo-American thought was not particularly receptive to the more or less alien idiom of a Comte or a Marx, but the views they championed would nevertheless reach English and American shores through the efforts of fellow travelers and acolytes. The work of John Stuart Mill is representative.

The youthful Mill was enchanted by the St. Simonians and Comte and ultimately emerged as a militant advocate of their new religious worldview. In 1841 Mill converted to Comte's Religion of Humanity, which was remarkably similar in substance to the nontheological utilitarianism of Jeremy Bentham, Mill's first "religion."[44] Henceforth he never wavered in his passionate commitment to replace Christianity with a Religion of Humanity. Mill is conventionally regarded as a secular thinker who championed ethical naturalism in contrast to traditional supernatural (theistic) ethics. Although he did champion what he called "purely human" ethics over against what he called "theological" ethics, Mill was very far from a secular thinker, if secular is defined as areligious or indifferent to religion. Throughout his life Mill pursued what can only be regarded as a religious mission. In a letter to Comte, Mill recounts the spiritual transformation he experienced upon reading Comte's *Cours*, an experience

---

[44] J. S. Mill, *Autobiography* (Penguin, 1990).

indistinguishable from religious conversion.[45] Mill explains:

> Having had the rather rare fate in my country of never having believed in God, even as a child, I always saw in the creation of a true social philosophy the only possible base for the general regeneration of human morality, and in the idea of Humanity the only one capable of replacing that of God. But there is still a long way from this speculation and belief to the manifest feeling I experience today—that it is fully valid and that the inevitable substitution [of Humanity for God] is at hand.[46]

Such an experience committed Mill to a two-pronged and lifelong goal: the evisceration of Christianity and social establishment of the Religion of Humanity he adopted, with revisions, from Comte. Mill, like St. Simon and Comte, bent his prodigious talents and will to the progressive elimination of Christianity from society and its replacement with a secular, social, or this-worldly religion.

---

[45] Voegelin has described Comte's writing of the *Cours* as a "spiritual practice," an insight supported both by Mill's method of absorbing the material and his intense response to it. Mill meditated long and hard on the work. As he told Comte, it was ". . . by successive rereading's of your work at my leisure . . . [that] I reached my final and decisive conception [of it] that was not only stronger but essentially new, since it is primarily of a moral nature." He discovered that Comte "had sown in the previous volumes such fertile seeds for all the main concepts of the last that even the most extraordinary ideas I read there seemed like friends I had always known" (*Corr*, 118). Mill's deep immersion in the *Cours* seems akin to the "spiritual practice" Comte himself undertook in writing the work.

[46] J.S. Mill, *The Correspondence of J.S. Mill and Auguste* Comte (New Brunswick: Transaction, 1995).

One consequence of such efforts was the insinuation of the radical anti-Christianity of the French secular messiahs into Anglo-American consciousness. Mill, who characterized his views as those of "advanced liberalism," is a pivotal figure in the transformation of classical to modern liberalism. An examination of his religious thought and aims is thus helpful in understanding the course of American social and political development over the past century, a development profoundly shaped by modern-liberal progressivism.

The first crucial issue concerns the meaning of a Religion of Humanity. The traditional God of the West is of course understood as both the ultimate Source of existence and value, and the ultimate End or goal of human existence (eternal salvation). The Religion of Humanity replaces God so conceived with the "Great Being" of Humanity. In other words, "Humanity" is henceforth to be regarded as the ultimate source of value and the ultimate end of human aspiration. The traditional religious obligation to serve God is replaced by the religious obligation to serve the intramundane abstraction Humanity, an obligation that becomes nothing less than the "law of our lives." Religious fulfillment is to be sought not in union with God but rather with Humanity, with one's fellow men, here and now, in this world. Indeed all religious yearning and impulse is to be reoriented away from the "baseless" conception of a transcendent God and toward the Great Being of Humanity. The Christian aspiration for immortality (vertical transcendence) is to be replaced by concern for the welfare of future generations on this earth (horizontal transcendence). Only the selfish, Mill says, will continue to yearn for personal immortality beyond this world; the morally cultivated will achieve fulfillment in knowing that their efforts live on in the well-being of future generations. Mill, following St. Simon and Comte, unequivocally proclaims the humanistic "religion without a God" vastly superior to any form of transcendent religion. All the secular messiahs universally and vigorously asserted the authentic and superior spirituality of secular to transcendent religion. The Religion of Humanity, Mill says, is not only a "real" religion but better and "more profoundly religious" than anything heretofore called by that name.[47]

A second important aspect of the Religion of Humanity or secular humanism concerns morality and law, and, in particular, its source. The traditional Judeo-Christian God is of course regarded not only as the source and end of existence but also of the moral law. The profound significance of the Judeo-Christian conception of the "higher law" for the development of Western constitutionalism, limited government, and the rule of law has been well documented by scholarly research.[48] The replacement of biblical with humanistic, naturalistic, or "purely human" ethics extirpates all such significance at a stroke, as does legal positivism, the philosophy of law that corresponds to such replacement. As Humanity supplants God as the ultimate source and end of value, so Humanity supplants God as the ultimate source of law. Upon social establishment of the Religion of Humanity Man and not God henceforth determines the nature and substance of law, moral and civil. "Theological" morality, as Mill says, is replaced with "purely human" morality, in his case, his particular version of Utilitarianism.

Utilitarianism, in Mill's hands, comes to resemble the social or altruistic morality devised by the St. Simonians and Comte and which also implicitly informs its English counterpart, the nontheological utilitarianism of Bentham.[49] It is seldom recognized that Benthamite

---

[47] Mill, *Utilitarianism*, 423.
[48] Edward S. Corwin, T*he Higher Law Background of American Constitutional Law* (Indianapolis: Liberty Fund, 2008).
[49] Ernest Albee, *A History of English Utilitarianism* (New York: Macmillan, 1957), 6.

utilitarianism, famously revised and disseminated by the Mills, was itself consciously intended to serve as a quasi-religious and naturalistic substitute for traditional Judeo-Christian morality. Bentham expressly acknowledged such an intention; as he said, "I suppose a new religion requires a new name: I propose utilitarianism."[50] The Benthamite religion embodies aspirations identical to those of the French secular messiahs. It too replaces service to God with this-worldly or temporal Service to Humanity (achieving the "Greatest Happiness of the Greatest Number . . . confined to the limits of this earth").[51] It too constructs a naturalistic or terrestrial ethics to replace the theological ethics that heretofore had governed Western civilization. The St. Simonians, Comte, Bentham, and Mill united in their efforts to ensure that henceforth Man and not God would govern this world.

Much of this history has been obscured or lost as a result of the vast social success of the anti-theological movements over the course of modernity. Many of the goals envisioned by the secular messiahs have been more or less realized, and the assumptions they embody are widely held in contemporary society as more or less self-evident truths. Traditional religion has largely been relegated to the sphere of private subjective belief, as Mill and others consciously intended. The tradition of the higher or natural law has been submerged in the rise of legal positivism and its variants. The moral has been supplanted by the social in many quarters; those who reject the moral obligation to Serve Humanity can only be regarded as selfish if not wicked. Altruism is widely championed even within nominally Christian circles. Significant numbers of persons in Western and American society have reoriented their religious aspirations away from a transcendent God and toward humanitarian service confined to the limits of

---

[50] Cited in Raeder, *Religion of Humanity*.
[51] Ibid.

the earth. The quasi-religious nature of the modern ideological movements such as socialism, fascism, and communism is well understood.[52] Millions of persons over the course of the past century channeled spiritual and religious aspirations into efforts to achieve a secular paradise on earth, whether conceived as the final communist or positivist state or the Kingdom of God of the Social Gospel. Through such efforts they hoped to find meaning and purpose in their existence, to achieve a kind of salvation through collective political action and reform. The hope, however implicit, was that such efforts would bring spiritual fulfillment. The hope, however implicit, was that union with Humanity would prove an existential substitute for union with God beyond this world, a God condemned as illusory by ideologues and fellow travelers.

Those who formulated or embraced one variant or another of the modern social or political religions clearly channeled what are self-evidently, and indeed self-avowedly, religious aspirations into the realization of ideals exclusively temporal. Such ideals—summarized by Mill as the "improvement of mankind"—were to be realized by moral, economic, and political reform and invested with religious—ultimate and salvific—significance and value. The religious valorization of worldly improvement, however, was not itself the ultimate goal of the various social messiahs and reformers but rather a by-product of their overarching end. The ultimate goal, in all cases, was the replacement of God with Humanity and theological with purely human, naturalistic, or secular morality of human construction. Voegelin and other scholars have characterized such aspirations, widespread in the nineteenth century, as attempts at the self-divinization of Man. We have seen Nietzsche's prophesy come to fruition: the replacement of God with Humanity did indeed lead to the redivinization of the state, the new Idol. Henri de

---

[52] See, for instance, Crossman, *The God That Failed*.

Lubac famously characterized the nineteenth century as enacting a "drama of atheist humanism," a drama unfolding to the present day.[53] Its players include not only the militant ideological movements but also their less virulent cousins such as the Social Gospel, American Progressivism, and the Religion of Secular Humanism.[54] All such actors embrace one variant or other of an intramundane Religion of Humanity that conceives human beings and not a transcendent God as the ultimate source and end of value.

The central tenets of modern secular humanism have been neatly summarized by J. Wesley Robb: "Man is his own rule and his own end."[55] Such a formulation succinctly expresses the twofold aims of the secular messiahs of the preceding centuries. *Man is his own rule*—morality is divorced from a transcendent source and henceforth regarded as of purely human construction. Such a conviction represents the triumph of the terrestrial or nontheological morality of the St. Simonians and Benthamites as well as the materialist morality of Marxism. The limits on human action entailed by the traditional notion of a law above the King—a God-given moral law superior to human preference—are abolished at a stroke. Man is entitled to construct whatever moral rules he chooses, in the spheres of both personal and political morality; he can become like God. *Man is his own end*: there is no goal or purpose to human existence beyond the subjective goals or values established by human beings. Humanity is an end-unto-itself. Man is free, as Nietzsche proclaimed, to "transvalue all values," to move Beyond Good and Evil, to exercise without restraint the "will to

---

[53] De Lubac, *Drama*.

[54] J. Wesley Robb, *The Reverent Skeptic: A Critical Inquiry into the Religion of Secular Humanism* (New York: Philosophical Library, 1979), 6.

[55] Ibid.

power."[56] No one can say the values of the Nazis or ISIS are inferior to the values of liberal democracy: man is his own rule and his own end.

The absurd and even demonic consequences of the modern drive to immanentization implicit in the modern political religions and related constructs are dramatically illustrated by the example of Auguste Comte, the founder of the Religion of Humanity. Comte went so far as to proclaim himself the new Christ, the "world-immanent last judge of mankind, deciding on immortality or annihilation for every human being."[57] The memory of those persons who had made significant intramundane contributions, he pronounced, would forever be preserved in the annals of mankind; indeed, the especially illustrious would be honored with a place in the Positivist "calendar of saints."[58] Such recognition was intended to serve as a this-worldly replacement for the immortality promised by Christian faith. Those who failed to make an enduring contribution to immanentist human welfare, on the other hand, were to be consigned to social oblivion; their memories would simply be erased from the records of human existence.

Comte's ideas, as we have seen, were taken seriously by many eminent persons, including Mill, one of the chief architects of modern-liberalism. Few scholars have explored either Mill's lifelong goal to replace Christianity with a Religion of Humanity or the relation between the new Humanitarian faith and modern-liberal progressivism. Voegelin is one of the few thinkers to have

---

[56] Walter Kaufman, *Nietzsche: Philosophers, Psychologist, Antichrist* (Princeton: Princeton University Press, 1974).

[57] William C. Harvard, "Notes on Voegelin's Contributions to Political Theory," in Ellis Sandoz, ed., *Eric Voegelin's Thought: A Critical Appraisal* (Durham, NC: Duke University Press, 1982), 131.

[58] Ibid.

done so. He draws attention to the relation between Comtean-Millian secular messianism and the ethos of secular liberal Progressivism, especially its ideal of ever-advancing immanentist Progress. Modern liberal Progressivism, he argues, manifests the existential imbalance characteristic of its virulent ideological brethren and is thus far less benign than generally believed. It impoverishes human existence by identifying progress with temporal material advance and obscuring the transcendent dimension of existence. Moreover, in relegating religious values to the private sphere of subjective preference, secular Progressivism creates a spiritual vacuum in the public square readily filled by messianic ideologues promising collective political salvation and ultimate fulfillment on earth. Voegelin warns, however, that the end of radically immanentist liberal progressivism is not the emergence of a realm of earthly perfection but rather the gulag and the concentration camp. As he starkly if colorfully puts it, the "progressivist symbolism of contributions, commemorations, and oblivion draws the contours of those 'holes of oblivion' into which the divine redeemers of the gnostic empires drop their victims with a bullet in the neck."[59]

Postmodernism, Multiculturalism, Tolerance

Over the past several decades American society has been engaged in what is popularly described as a "culture war," pitting secular "liberal" progressives against "conservative" traditionalists. The conflict is generally thought to involve various contested social issues, such as abortion, homosexuality and sexual expression more generally, education, the family, media, environment, and others. The focus on issue politics, however, tends to obscure the more fundamental and deeper divide in contemporary

---

[59] Ibid.

American society. Every culture is ultimately a product of the prevailing religious worldview held by members of that culture (*cultus*). The contemporary battle over the direction of culture in the United States is ultimately a battle not over discrete issues but rather conflicting religious worldviews. Modern liberal progressivism (the "Left') generally embodies the novel secular or human-centered faith that, as has been discussed, arose in competition to traditional biblical faith, generally defended by contemporary conservatism (the "Right"). The division between the two camps could not be starker. Their respective views conflict at the most fundamental level, the level of religion, encompassing as they do conflicting views regarding the very nature of human being and purpose of human existence. Nor could the stakes involved in the culture war be more significant. What is ultimately at stake is not the substance of particular public policy but rather preservation or destruction of the characteristically American way of life, dependent as it is upon certain inherited religious values (culture) implicit in both its institutional structure and customary practices.

The contemporary culture war is a particularly American manifestation of the general topic under discussion, that is, the modern revolt against God and displacement of Christianity by one variant or other of a secular or innerworldly political religion. Contemporary cultural and political conflict in the United States did not begin with recent elections but is rather an outcome of trends and movements developed over several centuries. The nineteenth century, as we have seen, witnessed the construction of various forms of intramundane social or political religion intended to supplant traditional Christianity. The political Left is the chief carrier of the novel secular religiosity in the American context, beginning with such movements as the Social Gospel and Progressivism, the proximate forebear of modern liberalism.[60] Traditional religious values and institutions are typically defended by the Right, the conservatives whose general aim, as the term indicates, is the conservation of traditional American values and institutions in the face of various modern challenges.

For well over a century the Left in both Europe and North America has led an assault on biblical religion and its civilizational manifestations. Such efforts have achieved substantial success; contemporary Western culture, including American culture, is saturated with the secular progressive worldview. The rising generation in the United States has been reared in a cultural environment profoundly shaped by nontheistic and even antitheistic assumptions, a society implicitly and explicitly informed by a post-Christian, post-theological, or postmodern worldview. Many members of American society are ignorant of the nature and history of Western civilization in general and American society in particular and increasingly unfamiliar with the religious worldview that impelled their development. The deracination of significant portions of the American populace, especially its younger members, may arguably be well-intended but is not accidental. It is rather the result of conscious efforts to transform American society, efforts typically spearheaded by secular or progressive elites. Advocates of such transformation, from Karl Marx through Antonio Gramsci to Saul Alinsky, have long understood that the success of their efforts depends upon transformation not only of particular political, economic, and legal institutions but culture more generally. As one prominent contemporary American public figure put it, such transformation requires a "change in our traditions, our

---

[60] Cashdollar, *Transformation of Theology*; Gillis Harp, *Positivist Republic*; Raeder, *Religion of Humanity*.

history."[61] Culture is always and everywhere the product of the cult (*cultus*). Thus the transformative change sought by the modern American Left necessarily involves transformation of the religious and moral self-understanding of traditional American society, an understanding decisively informed by biblical religion.

The ongoing transformation of traditional American values and beliefs has been facilitated by the rise of several significant intellectual and educational trends, among the most important of which are postmodernism, multiculturalism, and relativism. Marxism and related modern ideologies are widely recognized to have sought explicit transformation of Western society. The relation between the fashionable doctrines of postmodernism, multiculturalism, and relativism and the goal of cultural transformation is less commonly perceived. The means employed by the latter are more subtle, indirect, and implicit than those advocated by classic Marxist ideology, but such doctrines serve to undermine traditional Western and American society as surely, if not as straightforwardly, as Marxist doctrine proper. The English Fabians and fellow travelers were correct: the transformation of the free society in the direction of socialism or some other form of collectivism does not, as Marx suggested, depend on violent revolution. The same goal can be achieved by the gradual, evolutionary destruction of its foundational beliefs and values, as recognized by the British Fabians, their Progressive American counterparts, and later Communist strategists such as Gramsci. The realization of Communism, Gramsci maintained, requires destruction of the "cultural hegemony" putatively held by the capitalist

---

[61] "Barack knows that we are going to have to make sacrifices; we are going to have to change our conversation; we're going to have to change our traditions, our history; we're going to have to move into a different place as a nation." Michelle Obama, Speech given in San Juan, Puerto Rico on May 14, 2008.

ruling class—the false intellectual, philosophical, and religious ethos it has long perpetrated to maintain privilege and control. Such can be achieved by the patient and long-term reeducation of the populace within the framework of traditional social institutions, such as schools, universities, courts, and media. Communist student leader Rudi Dutschke famously reformulated Gramsci's evolutionary strategy as "the long march through the institutions."[62] We recall in this regard the motto of the Fabians: "Make Haste Slowly." Postmodernism, multiculturalism, and relativism are three gradualist or evolutionary means advanced by the modern Left toward attainment, surely if slowly, of its transformational goals.

Postmodernism

Postmodernism is the general term used to describe the overarching cultural perspective that develops in the West after the decline of "modernity." Scholars disagree on the precise origin of the term, variously attributing its first use to one or another nineteenth or early twentieth century thinker.[63] The central attribute of postmodern thought, on the other hand, is more readily identified, namely, skepticism toward or outright denial of the existence of universal or absolute Truth—a "Big T" Truth that transcends both history and the subjective values and

---

[62] In 1967, Dutschke, a German student leader, reformulated Gramsci's philosophy of cultural hegemony. Instead of a long military march, such as that undertaken by the Chinese Marxist Mao Tse-tung, the long march in the developed western nations would be through the most culturally significant of their social institutions—schools, universities, courts, and the popular media.

[63] The term originated as a critique of the putatively "modernist" scientific mentality of objectivity and progress associated with the French Enlightenment.

opinions of human beings. The Western tradition from classical Greece to modernity is of course saturated with the very outlook that postmodernism rejects—belief in objective and immutable Truth, including moral and religious Truth. Accordingly, the postmodern era, as previously noted, is often referred to as the "post-Christian" or "post-theological" era.

Postmodernism not only rejects the concept of absolute Truth but other conceptions central to the Western tradition as well. It rejects, for instance, the characteristic distinction between this-world and the world Beyond first apprehended by Plato, as well as the related distinction between nature (what is objectively given to humankind) and history (contingent human experience in time). On the postmodern view, Nature is more or less assimilated to History. Not only does the traditional concept of a given nature presuppose a metaphysical "Giver," which cannot be sustained on postmodern grounds, but the truth of nature can never be more than particular historical truth, the only form in which truth of any kind can or does exist. The postmodern restriction of truth to the various truths accepted by particular cultures and societies over time means of course that truth, like history itself, is continually in flux. Truth, as every other aspect of human existence in time, is and must be provisional and contingent, relative and conditional. What is true for postmodern society may not have been true for ancient or medieval society or, for that matter, the eighteenth-century society of colonial America. What is true for one culture, say Western culture, is not necessarily true for other cultures. What is true for one ethnic group may not be true for a different ethnic group. Indeed what is true for one person may not be true for a second person. There is no eternal and universal Truth that transcends particular historical truths, no absolute, unconditional Truth that transcends the relative truths of particular historical cultures, groups, individuals, and so on.

Postmodernism so conceived therefore must, and does, reject the Truth-claims associated with the Platonic and Judeo-Christian worldviews, and indeed any religion or philosophy that claims to articulate a universal or absolute Truth that transcends the movement of history. For postmodern thinkers, such truths as exist are inevitably subjective, relative, and conditional, relative to and contingent upon the particular perspective of the perceiver, a viewpoint generally described as "perspectivism."

Nietzschean Perspectivism

Various postmodern thinkers regard themselves as descendants of Friedrich Nietzsche, the German philosopher who famously announced the "death of God" at the close of the nineteenth century. Nietzsche's critique of Western civilization involved a thoroughgoing attack on the Platonic and Christian distinction between transcendence and immanence and the absolute Truth Platonism and Christianity claim to represent. According to Nietzsche, both conceptions are delusions or illusions. There is no Truth that transcends history, only the particular truths of particular perspectives. Nor is there a substantive reality transcending this world; remove the veil of illusion and one finds nothing but a void, a nothingness. The recognition of such hard truth, however, should not be met with despair but rather, Nietzsche proclaims, with courage and the will to create. The great majority of human beings, the weak and cowardly, will undoubtedly fall back on the comforting illusions of traditional philosophy and religion, but a few extraordinary individuals, the *Übermenschen* (Overmen or Supermen), possess the requisite courage and will squarely to face the truth of existence. The *Übermensch* responds to the metaphysical void not with despair but rather the realization that he himself must singlehandedly create the values, meaning, and purpose by which to orient his existence. Such are not given by God or a supernatural source, as Platonism and Christianity falsely maintain. Platonism and Christianity, again, represent mere illusions fit only to console and control the great mass of human beings, who, in fact, are little better than slaves. The Nietzschean *Übermensch* is superior to the mass. He alone does not flinch in the face of the void but rather accepts the challenge to endow his life with self-created value and purpose.[64] He alone has the strength to discard delusional crutches such as supernatural religion, suitable only for inferior human beings who lack the vitality and will truly to exist.

Nietzsche further maintains that the Truth-claims of Platonism and Christianity are not merely false and delusional but pernicious in yet another respect—they are hostile to life itself. Western philosophy and religion posit a transcendent realm in eternity and a transcendent morality to which man is obliged to align his values and action. According to Nietzsche, such conceptions diminish the significance of this world and existence in time. The negative rules of Judeo-Christian morality are especially malignant, compressing, restraining, and enervating the life force. Obedience to such rules makes man mild, meek,

---

[64] Elaborating the concept in *The Antichrist*, Nietzsche asserts that Christianity, not merely as a religion but also as the predominant moral system of the Western world, in fact inverts nature, and is hostile to life. "I call Christianity the one great curse, the one great intrinsic depravity, the one great instinct for revenge for which no expedient is sufficiently poisonous, secret, subterranean, and petty -- I call it the one immortal blemish of mankind. . . and one calculates time from the *dies nefastus* on which this fatality —arose— from the first day of Christianity! Why not rather from its last? From today? Revaluation of all values! Friedrich Nietzsche, Conclusion, *The Antichrist,* in Michael Tanner, ed, *The Twilight of the Idols and the Antichrist* (London: Penguin Classics, 1990).

passive—they make him slavish. Indeed, says Nietzsche, Christianity is the religion of slaves, its morality a "slave morality."[65] The *Übermensch* will not be constrained by such life-denying values. He rises up to "transvalue all values," to create his own morality and his own rules, "beyond Good and Evil."[66] He exerts what Nietzsche calls his "will to power"—his will to create his own existence.

According to Nietzsche, the metaphysical and religious tradition of Western civilization stemmed neither from disinterested search for Truth nor revelation by a supernatural God. It is rather a construction of human beings motivated by such a "will to power," the will to define or control reality through the creative act. Nietzsche generally employed the term in reference to the creativity of the artist. Certain of his descendants, most infamously the German Nazis, interpreted the will to power in a political sense, as the will to political power. Other postmodernists accept Nietzsche's critique of both metaphysics and absolute Truth—all truth is relative and conditional, dependent on the individual's perspective—but, unlike Nietzsche, tend to associate "perspective" with various neo-Marxist categories, especially the so-called "Marxian Trinity" of gender, race, and economic class. The truth perceived by a poor black woman, for postmodernists, is different from the truth perceived by a rich white man; truth is perspectival, relative, and conditional.

Postmodern theorists suggest, moreover, that the dominant traditions and values of Western civilization—Judeo-Christian morality, constitutionalism, the rule of law, capitalism—rose to dominance not because they are inherently true, in accord with nature, or conducive to

---

[65] Ibid.

[66] Friedrich Nietzsche, *Beyond Good & Evil: Prelude to a Philosophy of the Future*, trans, Walter Kaufman (New York: Vintage, 1989).

human flourishing. Such "social constructions" were rather invented or devised by those persons or groups that historically wielded power in society and this for the purpose of controlling or "marginalizing" less powerful persons and groups. Indeed postmodernists believe that the power possessed by cultural and political elites in all eras includes the power to define language itself, which in turn has enabled such groups to define truth and reality itself. In the case of Western civilization, its dominant elites—more or less European white men—putatively exercised their power to define language to cast themselves as superior to those groups over whom they wielded power—ethnic minorities, women, homosexuals, and other groups historically portrayed as culturally or socially inferior. The similarity to Marxism, which attributes the power to form a culture's prevailing ideas and values to the capitalist ruling class, and for the exclusive benefit of that class, is striking and obvious.

Indeed, for staunch postmodernists, the entire Western Canon—the classics of literature, philosophy, religion, art, music, and other cultural expressions that traditionally formed the basis of higher education in the West— represents little more than the biased and self-serving perspective of the powerful. The power of white European men enabled them to define the very concepts of "superior" and "inferior" and do so in a manner that ensured the continuing power of their own class and kind. This explains why Shakespeare, for instance, has long been included in the Western Canon but Hildegard von Bingen, the female medieval writer and polymath, has not. Shakespeare was a white European man and his elevation simultaneously elevated all white European men; female writers, on the other hand, were marginalized, relegated to insignificance. This is why Plato has traditionally been more highly regarded than the Greek lesbian poet Sappho. White heterosexual men held the power to define what is of value and what is not, and Plato served their purposes far better than Sappho. In postmodernist reality, however, objective grounds for holding Shakespeare superior to Hildegard or Plato superior to Sappho simply do not exist. Such a conclusion follows from the postmodern rejection of objective trans-historical standards, the only means by which such judgments could be made. Who is to say that Plato is superior to Sappho? Who is to say that Beethoven is superior to Madonna? Who is to say that the Mona Lisa is superior to Mickey Mouse or Antigone to American Idol? Who is to say that Notre Dame Cathedral is more beautiful than a strip mall? No one can make such claims. There is no absolute truth or objective universal standard that permits judgments of absolute superiority and inferiority. There is only subjective perspective—only your opinion and my opinion. All opinions are equally based on personal perspective, and all opinions are equally valid. The traditional definitions of superiority and inferiority are mere self-serving inventions or social constructions of dominant elites or power-holders, typically, in the West, white men. Such definitions and judgments have nothing to do with truth but only the will to power.

Such postmodern logic extends beyond artistic judgments to morality, law, politics, economics, science, religion, and every other cultural phenomenon.[67] Who is to say that marriage should be defined as a union between a man and a woman? Who is to say that Christianity is superior to Wicca? Who is to say that women should be permitted to drive an automobile, travel, and receive an education? Who is to say that it is always morally wrong to steal or kill or lie? Who is to say that rationality is better than irrationality? Who is to say that scientific laws capture objective truth? No one, according to postmodernism, can make such absolute judgments. Even the valorization of

---

[67] Postmodernism challenges the very concept of logic, regarded as yet another imposition of European man on other perspectives.

rationality and science represents only another "privileged" perspective posing as Truth. Who is to define freedom, justice, rights, law, and other terms of Western political discourse? Who is to say that the rule of law is superior to the personal rule of men? Who is to say what the U.S. Constitution means? Who is to say that capitalism is superior to socialism? Again, no one can make such claims, for there is no objective trans-historical standard by which to evaluate competing perspectives. Even theory and history—reason and experience—are mere perspectival constructs without universal validity. For postmodernists, traditional definitions and standards, including the standards of rationality, logic, and evidence, do not capture the truth of experience but merely further the power of historically dominant elites. Arguments and evidence offered by scholars and scientists, no matter how scrupulously constructed, can hold no more claim to objective truth than the assertion that Beethoven is superior to Madonna. Scholarship and science, like all claims to truth, in fact and necessarily merely evidence the subjective perspective of the researchers and, indeed, may serve merely to oppress and suppress dissenting perspectives.

Postmodernism thus poses a radical challenge to the foundational principles of Western civilization in general and American society in particular. Western civilization developed precisely on the basis of beliefs, values, and convictions rejected out-of-hand by postmodern doctrine. From the Greeks to the Americans, Western thought and practice was oriented by an ideal of objective Truth, whether the Forms of Platonism or the Divine Truth revealed by the biblical God, a Truth conceived as absolute, immutable, and universal, transcending history and particular perspective. Man, the rational animal of the Greeks, the rational persona of the Romans, the being endowed with reason of the Judeo-Christian conception, was believed not only equipped with reason but more or less obliged to employ that faculty to uncover Truth, moral and natural. Such truth as is discoverable by human reason was supplemented in the Platonic conception by the truth apprehended by mystical insight and, in the Christian conception, by the Truth revealed in Scripture. Throughout the course of its development, Western society not only conceived the objective reality of Truth but regarded its pursuit as worthy, legitimate, and even obligatory. Indeed Aristotle regarded the contemplative life in pursuit of truth (*theoria*) as itself the Highest Good, the *summum bonum*, as the medieval world would later describe it, a belief he bequeathed to the Western world that followed in his footsteps.

Western civilization developed upon the ancient conviction of the objective and immutable Truth of the order of existence. Such includes the conviction of an objective and immutable order of law—the moral and physical laws of nature which man can potentially discover or recognize but which he himself does not construct or invent. It developed upon the belief that certain actions are intrinsically moral or immoral, right- or wrong-in-themselves, regardless of an individual's subjective opinion, preference, or perspective. It developed upon the further belief in an objective or given human nature that is not susceptible of human or social construction. It developed on the belief that there is a superior, higher form of existence suitable to human nature and an inferior, lower form of existence that violates that nature. Certain actions or ways of life are in accord with the unfolding of human nature and certain ways of life prevent the realization of that nature. Postmodernism denies the Truth-value of all such traditional Western convictions, dismissing them as mere privileged and self-interested perspectives of the dominant elites who invented them. In so doing, postmodernism takes aim at the very heart and soul of Western civilization.

Multiculturalism

One of the major carriers of postmodernist thought in contemporary American society is the fashionable doctrine of Multiculturalism embedded in the greater part of educational curricula throughout the United States. The term itself is inoffensive and even appealing by traditional standards. Western educational aspirations generally included the expansion of intellectual and imaginative horizons beyond the limited confines of a student's particular culture, the hope of learning from experience and wisdom embodied in other historical civilizations. The goals of contemporary Multiculturalism, however, are of an entirely different nature. Multicultural education furthers a purpose quite unlike that of traditional cultural studies—a social and political purpose that involves, indirectly if not directly, the evisceration if not destruction of Western civilization. The seemingly benign banner of Multicultural education may prove to veil a Trojan Horse, offering putative gifts that prove pernicious if not disastrous in the long run.

The threat to Western society posed by the doctrine of Multiculturalism is most clearly perceived in light of the preconditions of cultural and social survival. Most persons, quite understandably, tend to assume that the society into which they are born will last forever: "There'll always be an England!" sang the British people in 1939.[68] Few persons ponder the origins of their own society or concern themselves with the means of its preservation and vitality.

---

[68] "There'll Always Be an England" is an English patriotic song, written and distributed in the summer of 1939, which became highly popular upon the outbreak of World War II. It was composed and written by Ross Parker (born Albert Rostron Parker, 16 Aug 1914 in Manchester) and Hugh Charles (born Charles Hugh Owen Ferry, 24 Jul 1907 in Reddish, Stockport, Cheshire).

Even a cursory study of human history, however, clearly demonstrates that societies and civilizations are not permanent, self-sustaining entities guaranteed to endure over time but transitory phenomena that rise and fall, appear and disappear, come and go. Contemporary societies and civilizations, including American society, are not exempt from the possibility that they too will one day be relegated, as is said, to the "dustbin of history." They are no more immune to the threat of historical decline than now-vanished civilizations of the past. American society, like all societies, is a fragile growth whose existence and flourishing require cultivation and care. Failure to recognize or honor the conditions of its existence and vitality may unintentionally lead to its demise. Civilizational decline or destruction can occur, moreover, not only through carelessness or ignorance but also willful intention. Insofar as the latter holds true, a society may not only experience cultural decline but also be said to commit cultural suicide.

Contemporary Multiculturalism is a popularized offshoot of postmodernist thought. Both constructs embrace radical relativism, perspectivism, and a denial of universal Truth that transcends particular historical experience. Multicultural education, as said, purports to serve an important and unobjectionable purpose—to expose American students to cultural beliefs and values beyond their immediate range of experience. Such exposure is considered necessary, among other reasons, to overcome a putative American ethnocentrism—an exclusive focus or preoccupation with the American cultural perspective. The aim of multicultural education is often widened to include a critique of so-called "Eurocentrism"—the exclusive focus on the values and perspective of Europe, the home of Western civilization and mother of America. The actual content of multicultural curricula, however, does not typically involve the praiseworthy goal of exposing students to the achievements of other historical cultures. Multicultural education rarely includes exploration of, say, Confucian China, Shinto Japan, the Byzantine Empire, or the ancient civilizations of Egypt and India. Students generally learn very little about the actual historical experience of other world cultures. What they unfailingly "learn" is rather the postmodernist dogma that all cultural perspectives are relative. They learn that no objective standard exists by which to evaluate the contributions of various cultures to world civilization and thus no civilization may be regarded as intrinsically superior or inferior. They learn that there is only "your culture" and "my culture," your cultural perspective and my cultural perspective; one is as valid as the other. Any judgments to the contrary merely evidence a pernicious American or European ethnocentrism. They learn, moreover, that an exclusive commitment to the values of one's own culture—a conviction that its values are good, perhaps even superior to those of other cultures, and thus worthy of defense—is not merely ethnocentric but indeed the gravest of all multicultural sins: the sin of "intolerance."

The willful imposition of Multiculturalist dogma in contemporary educational institutions not only serves the intended transformation of American culture desired by its advocates but, insofar as it achieves its goals, can only be regarded as attempted cultural suicide. In the name of Multiculturalist value-constructions such as "diversity," "otherness," and "tolerance," students are steeped in a philosophy of radical cultural relativism. The road of relativism is anticipated to end in the glorious embrace and celebration of "diversity." The more probable end, however, is nihilism (nothingness). If all cultures—all values, beliefs, and practices—are equally and relatively true, then nothing is True. The multiculturalist claim inevitably undermines commitment to one's own particular culture, conceived as merely one alternative among many equally valid options. In light of multiculturalist assumptions, efforts to preserve one's particular society, one's particular way of life, seem misguided if not absurd. Radical cultural relativism undermines a society at its deepest level, the level of self-preservation.

Such a possibility calls call for reflection upon the general conditions essential to the preservation of any culture, society, or civilization. We have discussed the fact that every society ultimately manifests the implicit and explicit beliefs, values, and assumptions—the worldview—embraced by its members. Society is man writ large, and man is a being that seeks value fulfillment. The values jointly held and pursued by members of a particular society largely generate the facts of that society, a relation derived from the nature of things.[69] Although it may seem obvious and self-evident, it must nevertheless be emphasized that the first and most basic requisite of cultural survival is the desire of a people to maintain the values and beliefs that constitute their culture's foundation and spring of action. A people indifferent to the characteristic values of their culture, or a people weary of existence, will lack the will to sustain it. An apathetic people will not put forth the effort that may be required to preserve their way of life, especially in the face of opposition from competing cultural paradigms. Such is also true of a people who, for one reason or another, grow hostile to their own culture, who come to denigrate or despise its customary values, beliefs, and practices. They may become convinced that their way of life is bad or wrong, detrimental to the planet or the flourishing of other cultures. Or they may simply be distracted, ignorant, or lazy, unwilling to expend the energy necessary to understand themselves or the larger culture of which they are part.[70] They may be unaware of

---

[69] "Values generate facts," in the words of F. A. Hayek.

[70] Neil Postman, *Amusing Ourselves to Death: Public Discourse in the Age of Show Business* (London: Penguin Books, 2005).

their own personal values and beliefs or those characteristic of their own culture. In such a case, they would be unable to recognize an attack on those values and thus disarmed from their defense.

The first condition for the survival of any society, then, is the conviction in the minds of the people that their particular society is worth preserving, that its characteristic values and beliefs are good and true, not merely relatively but absolutely. A people who despise themselves, hold themselves in contempt, or otherwise reject the enduring validity of their characteristic cultural values cannot and will not strive to preserve them. Such a conclusion seems self-evident. Thus one certain way to destroy a society is to convince the people that their society and culture, their way of life, is not good or special or grounded in Truth. Such is precisely the achievement of postmodern Multiculturalism.

Tolerance

Among the virtues preached by the gospel of Multiculturalism, perhaps none is accorded greater reverence than the virtue of "tolerance." On its face, the promotion of tolerance, like the promotion of multiculturalism, is unobjectionable and even praiseworthy. Both the virtue of tolerance and multicultural education have long been characteristic Western values. Multicultural tolerance, however, like contemporary Multicultural education in general, has little in common with the traditional Western virtue beyond a shared name. Tolerance is yet another characteristic Western value whose meaning has undergone significant transformation over recent decades. The traditional definition of tolerance, according to Merriam-Webster, is the "capacity to endure pain or hardship; sympathy or indulgence for beliefs or practices differing from or conflicting with one's own." In other words, throughout most of Western history, tolerance has implied "putting up" with something that causes one pain, enduring something that one personally dislikes or of which one personally disapproves. A person does not "tolerate" beliefs or behavior that he enjoys or finds praiseworthy but rather those he finds somehow offensive or repugnant. In the social and political sphere, tolerance thus means permitting other people to think and behave in ways that one personally finds objectionable, distasteful, or even morally wrong.

Tolerance so conceived has long been recognized as a Judeo-Christian virtue and enjoined on Christian conscience. Its classic Anglo-American defense was provided by John Locke in his celebrated work on religious freedom, *A Letter Concerning Toleration* (1689). Locke's work was inspired by the bloody conflict engendered throughout Western Europe in the aftermath of the Protestant Reformation, and, particularly, the English Civil War. Monarchs of the era claimed the right to control the religious beliefs of the populace. Religious division among the populace led various sects to fight long and hard to obtain political power, which was routinely employed to penalize members of dissenting sects. Locke identified the ultimate source of such religious conflict and violence—the claimed right of government to control the religious life of the people. The only way to end the violence, he said, was to remove the sphere of religion from political control. Religion and the Church, he said, should be recognized as voluntary associations and thus immune to the coercive reach of government. Religious sects must forego the use of coercion and agree to tolerate—put up with—one another's differences.

Toleration did not emerge in a spirit of graciousness or nobility but rather as a practical solution to the conflict of the era. The Western valorization of tolerance may have emerged as a pragmatic resolution of religious conflict but its significance extends far beyond religion and practical politics. Beyond securing peace, which of course is no mean accomplishment, the question is why persons should strive to be tolerant of thought, speech, and practice they dislike and perhaps even condemn, not only with respect to religion but social life more generally. Contrary to Multicultural teaching, the moral obligation of toleration in Western civilization, religious and otherwise, is not an autonomous or primary obligation but rather secondary and instrumental. The demand for toleration derives, in the end, from commitment to a higher and more fundamental Western value, namely, the primary value of human freedom. Members of Western society are obliged to tolerate much that they may personally dislike because such is a price of individual freedom. Every individual desires to be free to act on the basis of his personal values and purposes, values and purposes that others may find distasteful, offensive, or immoral. Every individual wants other persons to "put up with" his personal beliefs and idiosyncrasies. To recognize that one's personal desire for toleration is shared by all other human beings is to live by the Golden Rule. Justice—equality under law—demands that toleration of one's own beliefs and behavior be extended to equal toleration of others' beliefs and behavior.

Moreover, in a free society on the American model each individual is held to possess a natural right to liberty, that is, to engage in voluntary actions that do not violate the equal rights of other individuals. The only behavior legitimately restrained by law is behavior that violates other persons' unalienable rights to life, liberty, and property, including related First-Amendment rights such as free speech and free exercise of religion. Such rights do not include the right to be free from merely offensive or objectionable behavior, behavior of which one personally disapproves but which violates no one's natural or constitutional rights. Individual freedom so conceived thus obliges every individual to tolerate, put up with, beliefs and behavior he or she may find objectionable, so long as such behavior does not infringe on the legitimate rights of another person.

Such, however, is emphatically not the understanding of tolerance propounded by contemporary Multiculturalism. As one contemporary dictionary succinctly defines the novel Multicultural meaning, toleration is said to be "a disposition to tolerate or *accept* people or situations (emphasis added).[71] The concept of toleration has been transformed from "bearing," "enduring," or "putting up with" objectionable behavior to "accepting" such behavior. Such is not a superficial but rather profound change that fundamentally redefines the meaning of toleration. Moreover, such is the meaning that saturates contemporary American culture. Members of contemporary society have been taught, explicitly and implicitly, to identify "toleration" and "acceptance," a lesson conveyed by both popular culture and formal education at every level, from kindergarten to post-doctoral training. To tolerate is to accept, without judgment. Such is without question the meaning attached to the concept of toleration by the overwhelming majority of contemporary university students.

They have further been taught that "intolerance" so conceived, that is, the failure to accept—to express disapproval of the beliefs or behavior of other people—is among the most reprehensible of social crimes. Negative moral judgments are unpardonable, the very height of intolerance. A classic example is the issue of homosexuality. In the current cultural environment, persons dare not express moral disapproval of homosexual behavior, a disapproval, it should be noted, which has been more or less the norm within Western civilization since the ascendancy of Christianity. Multicultural toleration, however, means acceptance, without judgment, in this case to regard homosexuality as merely one lifestyle among

---

[71] The Free Dictionary.

various morally equivalent possibilities. Multicultural "tolerance" is thus related to other contemporary illiberal phenomena such as "political correctness," campus "speech codes," "hate speech," and the like. Even to think in traditional moral categories is condemned as wrong; indeed, such thought may be evidence of mental disease— "homophobia," "Islamophobia," and so on. Under such cultural pressure few persons are foolish or courageous enough to express conventional moral judgments or even employ common sense (consider, for instance, the contentious issue of "profiling" airline passengers).

Many college students and other young adults have been exposed to such a closed and repressive mental atmosphere since birth. One consequence is a disturbingly passive generation that seems incapable of making, certainly reluctant to make, moral judgments of any kind. Young people have been taught that to make such judgments is "intolerant" of other "perspectives." Self-censorship has become habitual among students shaped by Multicultural education, the mind unfamiliar with conceptual and moral discrimination.[72] To exercise the capacity for critical evaluation—to "judge"—is regarded as wrong, intolerant. (The irony of such strident moral condemnation of "intolerance" is striking: young people, largely forbidden to make moral judgments, have no difficulty condemning "intolerance" in no uncertain terms.) All behavior, all opinions, all cultures, must be regarded as more or less equal, relative to the individual's perspective. No one is

---

[72] The word "discrimination" has itself undergone transformation under the Multicultural dispensation. Contemporary usage tends to equate it with "prejudice" and injustice, implying that discrimination is always morally wrong. Merriam-Webster, however, retains the older definition, in which discrimination is defined as "the ability to recognize the difference between things that are of good quality and those that are not."

able or entitled to say that certain beliefs and actions are absolutely right or wrong or that certain cultural norms are superior to others. Such judgments are dismissed as mere "opinion"; others may hold a different opinion. There is no objective standard by which to judge between conflicting opinions and, in any case, to make moral or truth judgments would be intolerant.

Diversity

Students are implicitly taught that beyond tolerance (approval), the primary and absolute value, exists only the correlative value of "diversity"—the putative celebration of various and different perspectives and experiences, of "otherness." The Multicultural conception of diversity, however, requires as careful analysis as its corresponding conception of tolerance. American society has traditionally represented one of the most authentically diverse societies in the course of human history. Between 1782-1956, the de facto motto of the United States, as every schoolchild once learned, was *"E pluribus Unum"*—"out of many, One."[73] During the Founding era, the motto generally referred to the welding of a single federal political order out of many individual political communities—originally colonies and then states united under the federal Constitution. Over time, however, it acquired further significance for American self-understanding. America, as the saying goes, is a "nation of immigrants," a "melting pot" enriched, one might say, by the diverse perspectives of people from a variety of cultural and ethnic backgrounds. American society is atypical for many reasons, among which is the lack of relation been American

---

[73] *E Pluribus Unum* had been adopted by an Act of Congress in 1782 as the motto for the Seal of the United States and has been used on coins and paper money since 1795. Few of my undergraduate students have ever heard of the phrase.

identity and kinship or ethnicity. American identity is not a function of birth or biology but rather of commitment to certain general or abstract values and principles. American identity, unlike national or cultural identity in the majority of societies known to history, is not defined by race, ethnicity, or biological factors of any kind. Any person, from any ethnic or cultural background, can, in principle, be an American. The only requirement is the acceptance of certain value commitments, in particular, the moral and political principles that underlie the unique structure of American constitutional order. "One, from Many": the "Many" is inseparable from the "One"—the unity of moral and political principle that makes the diverse "Many" one people, the American people.

The traditional economic order of American society further promotes a truly diverse society. Capitalism not only permits but encourages multiplicity—diversity of tastes, interests, and pursuits. The abstract legal framework comprised by the rule of law serves the same purpose. Law does not command individuals to pursue specific values or ends but merely structures the means they must employ in pursuing their diverse personal values and purposes. Indeed the hallmark of the free society is pluralism—the pursuit of diverse and individually self-determined values and goals and not a unitary purpose binding on every individual. A pluralistic society such as traditional America honors the fact that values and purposes vary greatly among persons and does not recognize a right of government to impose a uniform set of goals on the populace. The traditional American ideal—morally, legally, politically, economically—has long been diversity-within-unity, *e pluribus unum.*

American universalism—the conception that any person can in principle be an American—is yet another manifestation of the underlying Judeo-Christian vision that informs traditional American political order. Christian universalism teaches that all human beings share the same nature and possess equal spiritual worth, a worth that does not derive from their particular attributes but rather human nature itself: "There is neither Jew nor Greek; there is neither slave nor free; nor is there male and female, for you are all one in Christ Jesus" (Galatians 3: 28). A person is not defined by what might be called "secondary attributes" (concrete particulars such as ethnicity, gender, and so on) but rather his essential nature or substance, his abstract status as a human being.

Contemporary Multiculturalism dramatically revises such traditional American ideals. More particularly, it eviscerates the elements of unity and universalism bound up with traditional American self-understanding. The Multiculturalist perspective recognizes only "the Many"— "diversity," "difference," and "otherness"—and turns a blind eye toward a shared and unifying "One." Indeed it challenges and even rejects the view that American identity is defined by subscription to unifying moral and political principles. Such a view is dismissed, even reviled, as mere American ethnocentrism, regarded as yet another means by which dominant elites, including the Founders themselves, marginalize and suppress persons and groups who do not subscribe to traditional American principles and values. To assert allegiance to values such as constitutionalism, the rule of law, unalienable natural rights, and economic freedom is to assert a merely subjective opinion and, moreover, display "intolerance" of diversity and difference. We recall that both Postmodernism and Multiculturalism challenge or reject the concept of objective and universal Truth; such truth as exists is merely relative and perspectival. On such a view, American founding principles certainly do not represent an objective and abiding truth of existence. Such principles, as previously noted, are little more than historical relics or, worse yet, mere social constructions of the powerful that serve to silence the voices of less powerful groups. Indeed they are hardly more than mere "American propaganda."[74]

There is no more reason to honor such social constructions than the equally oppressive social constructions of Christianity, which similarly serve to suppress the perspectives of historically marginalized social groups. Postmodern Multiculturalism regards all traditional concepts and views—gender roles, sexual preference, family structure, morality, constitutionalism, the rule of law, economic theory, and beyond—in the same light. There is no objective reality or Truth that validates the superiority of the traditional family or heterosexuality. Such concepts, like constitutionalism and the rule of law, are merely cultural constructs invented throughout history by dominant and self-serving elites. Language controls reality and those who hold power control language. There is no objective reality given to man that language serves to describe, only the social construction of meaning. Language is regarded as eminently plastic and malleable, readily susceptible to human design. Moreover, insofar as reality is little more than a social construction defined by language, the proper manipulation of language can serve to change or transform reality itself. Thus the ongoing redefinition of the meaning of the central moral and political concepts of traditional Western and American society discussed throughout this work. And thus the endless charade of postmodern politics, its twisting and parsing of language, fantastic promises, and absurd observations that defy reality. Indeed postmodern political actors in the United States frequently appear to be outright liars. Such a judgment, however, is not quite accurate. In order to lie, one must first believe in Truth, which postmodern politicians do not. They are postmodernists, which means they regard reality as plastic

---

[74] According to a university professor of my acquaintance, who would undoubtedly prefer to remain anonymous.

and formed by language. They further believe, as discussed, that he who has power—political power—controls language and thus reality. Thus the endless repetition of what appear as blatant untruths to members of society whose vision is informed by traditional ("pre-postmodern") presuppositions.

Postmodernism and Multiculturalism regard truth and reality as relatively meaningless concepts but attribute the greatest possible significance to language. Despite their intense preoccupation with language, however, such constructs fail to recognize one of the most important characteristics of language, which is not its role in the "social construction" of reality but rather transmission of the actual historical experience of a people. We have discussed the traditional American ideal of "diversity within unity." One requisite of achieving such unity among the culturally diverse members of American society is the acquisition of the historical language of that society—English. Contrary to postmodern assertions, the English language is not a constructed artifact but rather a spontaneously evolved carrier of cultural experience. To learn any language is simultaneously to learn a particular way of experiencing the world. In the case of the English language, it is to absorb the unique experiences that have shaped the development of Anglo-American society. An individual cannot fully understand or participate in American society (or any society) without understanding the language that carries its meaning. As any bilingual person will attest, to comprehend two languages is to perceive reality through two different lenses, to perceive two different worlds.

A common language is essential to a common culture, a fact long recognized in the United States. Historically, a primary goal of immigrants, if not for themselves then for their children, was to learn English, a goal also encouraged if not demanded by the larger culture—schools, churches, businesses, and so on. Postmodern Multiculturalism, however, dismisses the significance of language for cultural unity. Its proponents suggest, on the contrary, that to learn English is to be subjected to the ethnocentric social constructions of European culture, historically dominated by white Christian men and long serving to oppress women, homosexuals, people of color, non-Christians, and other minorities. Contemporary immigrants to the United States are rarely encouraged, indeed often implicitly discouraged, to learn its language, which is to say, absorb its traditions, values, and meaning. The absence of a shared language, however, eliminates an essential social bond. There can be no American people, no American society, without an element of unity, and a common language is central to such unity. The multicultural demand for diversity, extending even to language, can only shatter American society into disjointed fragments. Scholars warn of the "Balkanization" of America that looms large if present trends are not arrested.[75]

The assault on the English language, however, is merely one skirmish within the greater battle fought by postmodern multiculturalists—the battle against traditional American society and the overarching civilization from which it emerged. Multiculturalism is an important phenomenon because it embodies at a popular level numerous currents implicated in the ongoing erosion of American and Western culture. The free society emerged in Western Europe in line with the particular values, assumptions, beliefs, and historical circumstances of the European peoples. Over time the Judeo-Christian worldview blended with elements of Greco-Roman and Germanic culture to form the unique civilization of Christendom. The spiritual foundation of that civilization

---

[75] Merriam-Webster defines the primary meaning of Balkanization as follows: 1. To break up (as a region or group) into smaller and often hostile units.

comprises certain fundamental and related convictions, including the reality of a transcendent God who creates man in his image. Every human being is regarded as a being of inestimable spiritual worth, endowed with reason and free will, and charged with a profound personal mission—to earn eternal salvation. The biblical worldview further comprises a distinction between heaven and earth, this world and the world Beyond. It is also bound to the conviction of an omnipotent and omniscient God who is the source of order in existence, both natural and moral order, a God who rules the world providentially and administers ultimate divine justice in the world Beyond time. Western civilization is grounded on the belief in a creative Source who stands beyond history and who establishes the nature of things, the givenness of existence in this world.

The characteristic moral, legal, political, and economic practices and institutions of traditional American society presuppose all such convictions to varying degrees. Postmodernism dismisses all of them in one fell swoop. Indeed it dismisses the very concept of cultural, social, or spiritual "foundations," which implies a rootedness transcending the flux of history. It challenges the concept of Nature as an index of objective reality beyond the reach of human subjectivity. The postmodernist view perceives no such reality, no givenness of existence impermeable to human will and action. Nature is dismissed as yet another social construction, leaving behind only History, only human experience in time, only particular cultures, particular religious beliefs, particular historical circumstances, and so on. Natural or Higher Law recedes from view along with the concept of universal and overarching Truth, convictions central to the Western tradition for millennia. For postmodernists as for Progressives, truth, including metaphysical and religious truth, consists solely in the relative and particular truths thrown up by particular historical experiences in particular cultures.

Although postmodernism rejects foundationalism, not every postmodern thinker always and necessarily rejects the particular cultural experiences that constitute the Western and American tradition. Thinkers such as Richard Rorty defend certain traditional values not on the ground of truth-in-itself but rather on the ground of History.[76] The experiences and values that shaped Western civilization are recognized as definitive for American society, and insofar as the American people wish to preserve their way of life, says Rorty, they are obliged to honor them. Such values, however, cannot be regarded as representing the truth of reality but only relatively true—true for American or European society but not societies that developed on the basis of different cultural perspectives. Americans, then, are permitted to defend their particular society but only on the basis of History, not Nature or Truth. American traditions and values may be valid for Americans due to their particular historical experience but cannot be regarded as universally valid, true-in-themselves, or rooted in any foundation other than the vagaries of history. The majority of postmodern multiculturalists, however, are far less accepting of Western and American culture. They reject not only the concept of foundationalism, as does Rorty, but also the substantive values and traditions characteristic of Judeo-Christian civilization. Such values, as we have seen, are typically dismissed as self-serving social constructions of hegemonic elites who employ their power of controlling language to oppress or marginalize perspectives of the less powerful.

Many individuals who pursue the Multicultural agenda and educational curriculum undoubtedly do so on the

---

[76] Richard Rorty, *Achieving Our Country: Leftist Thought in Twentieth-Century America* (Cambridge: Harvard University Press, 1998).

basis of mere naivety or thoughtlessness, failing to consider either the sources or implications of such a paradigm. The doctrine, moreover, is not only popular and politically correct but a mandatory component of educational curricula in many public schools. Teacher training in the universities is saturated with Multicultural dogma, and public schoolteachers are often required to transmit its teachings regardless of their personal values or concerns. For various reasons, then, many advocates of Multiculturalism may be unaware that the doctrine is a spearhead of contemporary neo-Marxist movements in the United States and elsewhere. The leaders of such movements correctly perceive the utility of the Multicultural paradigm with respect to the fundamental transformation of Western society for which Marx once yearned and they themselves continue to yearn. We have mentioned the "long march through the institutions" anticipated by Gramsci and others.

Contemporary Multiculturalism, as previously observed, is not concerned with comparative study of various world cultures, as the term would imply. The actual content of Multicultural studies in the majority of American educational institutions is of Marxist inspiration, whether or not such is explicitly recognized or acknowledged. More particularly, the basic paradigm of postmodern Multicultural theory is saturated with the Marxian concept of class struggle. Postmodern thinkers, following Marx, tend to perceive class struggle or conflict—the conflict between oppressors and victims—as the essence of social relations. So-called cultural Marxists, however, move beyond Marx in broadening and extending that struggle beyond the economic antagonism between capitalist and worker to other dimensions of social experience as well, in particular, race and gender. The oppressors are generally portrayed as European elites of various kinds—"Dead White Men," such as the American Founders, who imposed their definition of reality on others. The victims comprise the myriad of putatively marginalized groups—women, people of color, Native Americans, non-Christians, homosexuals, non-western civilizations, and even the planet itself (endangered by Western science and greed). Indeed, on the Postmodern and Multiculturalist view, the very concept of civilization appears as a symbol of Western oppression, defined by powerful elites and imposed on those subject to their power. What is civilization or civilized behavior? Who is to say? The traditional meaning assigned in the West, like the meaning of its other traditional symbols, has no inherent validity but is merely one more language-construct foisted on the powerless by self-serving elites.

Postmodern Multiculturalism, as previously observed, drives a stake into the heart of Western civilization. All traditional concepts and values are transformed or transvalued, if not denigrated and reviled. Western standards have no claim to objectivity or Truth or superiority to other cultural standards; indeed, they have been unmasked as the symbols of oppression they always were. Similar judgements extend to every value and institution associated with the West, including its central conception of a universal human nature shared by all human beings. Multiculturalism replaces Christian universalism with an atavistic tribalism that conceives personal identity as bound to one's specific racial, cultural, or other particularistic group (race, gender, class). It is thus related to the rise of so-called "identity politics" in the United States, the demand for recognition and status asserted by the myriad groups putatively marginalized and oppressed by Western civilization. American college campuses have seen the development of African-American Studies, Women's Studies, Queer Studies, Latino Studies; and so on. College courses in Western Civilization have largely been eliminated or replaced by courses such as Eurocentrism. Students and others are encouraged to identify with their particularity and not a universally shared humanity. There is no such universal human nature, on the Multiculturalist view, but only particular cultural forms shaped by history.

Multiculturalism thus challenges the Judeo-Christian or Western conception of what it means to be a human being, with potentially profound consequences for American moral, legal, and political order. Traditional American institutions are inseparable from the conviction of a universal human nature. Such a conviction lies at the root of the Founders' declaration that "all men are created equal," endowed with identical individual rights, and entitled to be judged by identical laws. The postmodern rejection of a universal human nature thus leads, among other consequences, to rejection of the traditional American ideal of the rule of law. Legal theorists influenced by postmodern Multiculturalism have argued that particular groups should be ruled by particular laws unique to their particular circumstances and experiences. Judges are encouraged to take into account the particular cultural experiences of plaintiffs and defendants in reaching judicial decisions. Judges may even claim superior wisdom based upon their personal membership in a traditionally "marginalized" group. The recent and controversial remark of Supreme Court Justice Sonya Sotomayor—"I would hope that a wise Latina woman . . . would more often than not reach a better conclusion than a white male who hasn't lived that life"—is saturated with such postmodern Multiculturalist assumptions.[77] Calls have been made for incorporation of traditional Islamic Sharia law into the American system of justice. On the Multicultural viewpoint, such inclusion is perfectly

---

[77] "I would hope that a wise Latina woman with the richness of her experiences would more often than not reach a better conclusion than a white male who hasn't lived that life." Sonia Sotomayor, 2001 speech at Judge Mario G. Olmos Law and Cultural Diversity Lecture, University of California, Berkley.

sensible—particular communities should be ruled by their own particular law. Such a view, however, is in utter conflict with central values of the American system of justice—the general ideals of the rule of law and equality under law, the universal application of identical rules to all manner of persons, without distinction. The same may be said for the Multicultural argument that judicial decisions should take into account the particular cultural circumstances of litigants. Traditional America has insisted, on the contrary, that "Justice is Blind," that the law, like God, is no respecter of persons.

Multicultural relativism and perspectivism lead not only to an explicit rejection of the traditional American conception of justice but also traditional views of religion, morality, marriage and the family, sex roles and practices, and capitalism, indeed every value and institution historically associated with American society. The premises of postmodern Multiculturalism preclude the defense of any traditional value on any grounds but the vagaries of history, a defense which itself runs the risk of condemnation as both ethnocentric and intolerant. The proper attitude is to be tolerant (accepting) and open to otherness and diversity. The disparagement or rejection of traditional values extends even to patriotism, said to be yet another manifestation of ethnocentric hubris. Americans must learn to overcome parochial attachments to their way of life and become "global citizens," celebrating the equal value of all cultural perspectives. They must overcome their traditional attachment to Christianity. Biblical religion must be recognized as merely one perspective or subjective preference among others of equal validity. They must overcome their traditional commitment to capitalism, which is similarly disarmed from claiming the status of objective truth, representing, on the contrary, the "false consciousness" or mere rationalization of capitalist oppressors. The Founders' idea of unalienable rights, as mentioned, should be dismissed as mere propaganda.

History itself must be redefined, transformed, "changed." Conventional history represents not a true and accurate account of human experience but rather the selective and self-serving narrative of cultural and political elites. In the end, none of the values, beliefs, assumptions, traditions, institutions, or customs that constitute the traditional American way of life are left standing. The Fabian Socialists were right—violent revolution is far from necessary to transform and even destroy a society or indeed an entire civilization.

We thus return to the issue introduced at the outset—the issue of cultural survival. The fundamental requisite of such survival—the will to perpetuate one's particular culture—is difficult if not impossible to sustain in a society saturated with Multiculturalist assumptions. Contemporary Multiculturalism portrays all cultures as more or less equal and recognizes few if any intrinsic values beyond "tolerance-acceptance" and "diversity." Such doctrine inevitably undermines confidence in the worth of any particular way of life, including the American way of life. Americans are not entitled to regard their unique culture as anything more than one historical option among various others of equal validity. Such radical relativism and perspectivism inevitably weaken patriotic sentiment and the willingness or ability to defend traditional American values in the face of competing cultural constructs and worldviews. A people will only defend the characteristic values of their society if they believe they are good and worth preserving. Such conviction, however, is daily undermined by the explicit and implicit Multicultural message conveyed to members of American society, especially its youth, by both contemporary education and influential popular media. Indeed every dimension of contemporary American society—moral, religious, cultural, political, and historical—is saturated with the belief-complex or worldview of postmodern perspectivism and relativism.

A particular manifestation of the relation of Multiculturalism to the decline of American patriotism is its explicit denigration of the traditional notion of so-called American Exceptionalism.[78] From its inception, the American people generally regarded their new nation as unique among nations, charged with a special mission in accord with God's providential design. America, in the celebrated phrase of John Winthrop, was to be the "City upon the Hill," the shining example of a free people under God.[79] America was not like other nations, the overwhelming majority of which were founded on force and conquest. America was different, unique, exceptional. For the first time in history, human beings were given the opportunity to devise a constitutional order on the basis of rational reflection and not under pressure of force or compulsion. For the first time in history, human beings devised a political order that not only expressly acknowledged the equal worth of every individual but aimed to provide universal institutional protection of his unalienable rights, the moral treatment to which every individual is entitled by virtue of his human nature.[80]

On the view of postmodern Multiculturalism, American Exceptionalism so conceived can only appear preposterous, indeed precisely the kind of ethnocentric hubris Multiculturalism strives to overcome. Accordingly, Multicultural curricula often bombard students with a one-sided account of history that highlights the failures and flaws of the American experience. Students typically learn little about the actual historical circumstances and

---

[78] Charles Murray, *American Exceptionalism: An Experiment in History* (Washington, DC: AEI Press, 2013).

[79] Speech, John Winthrop, "A Model of Christian Charity," 1630.

[80] Preamble, U.S. Constitution

values that underlie the American founding or the significance of American achievements in world history. They learn instead that the Founders were slaveholders and oppressors, not only of African slaves but other marginalized groups such as women and Native American peoples. They learn little about the massive destruction of human life that resulted from the twentieth-century experiment with economic centralization (many have never heard of a gulag or a Mao Tse-tung), but are generally well acquainted with the so-called "Robber Barons" of the Gilded Age. They learn little about the laws of economics but are outraged by the "corporate greed" that permits Nike to pay Chinese workers a fraction of their American counterparts and persuaded that the propaganda of Michael Moore's "Sicko" is worth the attention of serious persons. They learn little or nothing of the contribution of biblical religion to the development of Western civilization and Western values, values they generally take for granted, but unfailingly learn that religious conviction is mere subjective opinion and preference. American college students know little of the actual content of the United States Constitution; indeed about sixty percent of them believe the Marxist slogan "From each according to their ability, to each according to their need" is contained therein. They learn little about the structure, function, or purpose of the American federal government but are nonetheless convinced that health care is a universal or human right. They learn nothing of the purpose or function of law yet are quite sure that the Supreme Court should be culturally diverse.

Multiculturalism is far from the only contemporary trend that poses a threat to the preservation of American society. Its special significance arises from its role as a carrier, in a simplified and seemingly benign manner, of neo-Marxist aspirations. Multiculturalism as practiced in contemporary American society shares the purpose if not the methods of the ideological movements of the twentieth century, namely, the transformation of Western and American society. The experience of Europe is most instructive in this regard. American Multiculturalism was largely imported from European sources. The doctrine has to date advanced further in its birthplace than in America, allowing a glimpse of its longer-term consequences. Relativistic *Toleranz* (acceptance) has become a more or less absolute value in many Western European nations, one that dare not be challenged, while contempt for the religious tradition that formed the basis of Western civilization knows few bounds. Despite pleas and protests from religious leaders, for example, European political leaders refused to acknowledge, even cursorily, the Christian roots of European civilization in the founding documents of the European Union. The decline of Christianity and accompanying rise of Multicultural "tolerance-acceptance" has disarmed European peoples from defending their traditional values and way of life in the face of non-European immigrants who do not share Western values. In recent years—the massive influx of Moslem migrants from the war-torn Middle East—the situation has become progressively more unwieldy and even dangerous. Farsighted European statesmen and scholars warn that the resulting inability to assimilate the large influx of immigrants from non-Western cultures such as fundamentalist Islam, whose religious worldview is both alien and antagonistic to that of the West, may lead to the disappearance of Europe as a distinct civilization, perhaps within the lifetime of present inhabitants.[81]

---

[81] There are recent signs that Western leaders are awakening to the dangers posed by Multiculturalism and related paradigms, for instance, the criticism of multiculturalism by David Cameron in England, Angela Merkel in Germany, and Nicolas Sarkozy in France; publications such as Marcello Pera, *Why We Should Call Ourselves Christians: The Religious Roots of Free Societies* (NY: Encounter Books, 2011) and Bruce S. Thornton,

Decline and Fall: Europe's Slow Motion Suicide (Encounter Books, 2007).

83

Bibliography

Acton, H.B. 2003. *The Illusion of the Epoch: Marxism-Leninism as a Philosophical Creed.* Indianapolis: Liberty Fund.

Billington, James. 1980. *Fire in the Minds of Men: Origins of the Revolutionary Faith.* New York: Basic Books.

Carey, George W. 1995. *In Defense of the Constitution.* revised and expanded. Indianapolis: Liberty Fund.

Cashdollar, Charles D. 1989. *The Transformation of Theology, 1830-1890.* Princeton: Princeton University Press.

Cohn, Norman. 1970. *The Pursuit of the Millenium.* New York: Oxford University Press.

Corwin, Edward S. 2008. *The Higher Law Background of American Constitutional Law.* Indianapolis: Liberty Fund.

Crimmins, James E., ed. 1990. *Religion, Secularization, and Political Thought: Thomas Hobbes to J.S. Mill.* London: Routledge.

Crossman, Richard H., ed. 2001. *The God That Failed.* New York: Columbia University Press.

Dostoyevsky, Fyodor. 1993. *The Grand Inquisitor: with Related Chapters from the Brothers Karamazov.* Indianapolis: Hackett Publishing Comany, Inc.

Ellul, Jacques. 1979. "Politization and Political Solutions." In *The Politicization of Society,* edited by Kenneth S. Templeton. Indianapolis: Liberty Press.

Evans, M. Stanton. 1994. *The Theme is Freedom: Religion, Politics, and the American Tradition.* Washington, D.C.: Regnery Publishing, Inc.

Franz, Michael. 1992. *Eric Voegelin and the Politics of Spiritual Revolt: The Roots of Modern Ideology.* Baton Rouge: Louisiana State University Press.

Frohnen, Bruce, ed. 2002. *The American Republic: Primary Sources.* Indianapolis: Liberty Fund.

Hall, Daniel L. Dreisbach and Mark David, ed. 2009. *The Sacred Rights of Conscience.* Indianapolis: Liberty Fund.

Hamburger, Joseph. 1999. *John Stuart Mill on Liberty and Control.* Princeton: Princeton University Press.Harp,

Gillis. 2005. *Positivist Republic: Auguste Comte and the Reconstruction of American Liberalism, 1865-1920* . University Park, PA: Penn State University Press.

Hayek, F.A. 1991. *The Fatal Conceit: the Errors of Socialism.* ed W.W. Bartley III. Chicago, University of Chicago Press.

Hegel, G. W. F. 1929. *Hegel: Selections.* Edited by Jacob Loewenberg. New York: Scribner's Sons.

Hoffer, Eric. 1951. *The True Believer: Thoughts on the Nature of Mass Movements.* San Bernardino: Borgo Press.

Koenker, Ernest B. 1965. *Secular Salvations: The Rites and Symbols of Political Religions.* Philadelphia: Fortress Press.

Locke, John. 2003. *Two Treatises of Government and a Letter Concerning Toleration.* New Haven: Yale University Press.

Lubac, Henri de. 1995. *The Drama of Atheist Humanism.* San Francisco: Ignatius Press.

Löwith, Karl. 1949. *Meaning in History.* Chicago: University of Chicago Press.

Manuel, Frank E. 1983. *The Changing of the Gods.* Hanover, NH: Brown University Press.

_____. 1956. *The New World of Henri Saint-Simon.* Cambridge: Harvard University Press.

Mazlish, Bruce. 1976. *The Revolutionary Ascetic: Evolution of a Political Type.* New York: McGraw-Hill.

Opitz, Edmund A. 1996. *Religion: Foundation of the Free Society.* Irvington-on-Hudson, NY: Foundation for Economic Education, Inc.

Orwell, George. 2010. *Politics and the English Language and Other Essays*. Oxford: Benediction Classics.

Pera, Marcello. 2011. *Why We Should Call Ourselves Christian*. New York: Encounter Books.

Pestritto, Ronald J. and William J. Atto, ed. 2008. *American Progressisvism: a Reader*. Lanham, MD: Lexington Books.

Pestritto, Ronald J. 2005. *Woodrow Wilson and the Roots of Modern Liberalism*. Lanham, MD: Rowman & Littlefield Publishers, Inc.

Raeder, Linda C. 2002. *John Stuart Mill and the Religion of Humanity*. Columbia, MO: University of Missouri Press.

Ryn, Claes G. 1992. "Political Philosophy and the Unwritten Constitution." *Modern Age* 303-309.

Sebba, Gregor. 1981. "History, Modernity, and Gnosticism." In *The Philosophy of Order: Essays on History, Consciousness and Politics,* edited by Peter J. Opitz and Gregor Sebba. Stuttgart: Ernst Klett.

Shah, Timothy Samuel and Hertzke, Allen D., ed. 2016. *Christianity and Freedom. Vol. I: Historical Perspectives.* II vols. Cambridge: Cambridge University Press.

Shaw, G. Bernard. 1889. *Fabian Essays in Socialism.* London: Fabian Society.

Smith, Ronald Gregor. 1966. *Secular Christianity.* New York: Harper and Row.

Sowell, Thomas. 1987. *A Conflict of Visions: Ideological Origins of Political Struggles.* New York: William Morrow & Co.

Talmon, Jacob L. 1960. *Political Messianism.* New York: Frederick A. Praeger.

_____. 1952. *The Rise of Totalitarian Democracy.* Boston: Beacon Press.

Thornton, Bruce S. 2007. *Decline and Fall: Europe's Slow Motion Suicide.* San Francisco: Encounter Books.

Turner, James. 1985. *Without God, Without Creed: the Origins of Unbelief in America*. Baltimore: Johns Hopkins University Press.

Viner, Jacob. 2015. *The Role of Providence in the Social Order: An Essay in Intellectual History*. Princeton: Princeton University Press.

Voegelin, Eric. 1986. *Political Religions*. Translated by T. J. DiNapoli and E.S. Easterly III. Edwin *Mellen Press*.

_____. *1968. Science, Politics, and Gnosticism*. Chicago: Henry Regnery Company.

Witte, John Jr. 2005. *Religion and the American Constitutional Experiment*. 2nd. Boulder: Westview Press.

Wright, T.R. 1986. *The Religion of Humanity: The Impact of Comtean Positivism on Victorian Britain*. Cambridge: Cambridge University Press.